Vera Mackay
July 1983.

The Hamlyn Book of
CROCHET

The Hamlyn Book of
CROCHET

From first stitches to fashion garments

Carol Payton

HAMLYN
London · New York · Sydney · Toronto

To Malcolm

The pattern for the Mother and Daughter Ponchos
on p.6 can be found on p. 73.

The pattern for the Boy's Set on p. 10
can be found on p. 57.

ACKNOWLEDGEMENTS

The author would like to thank Mary Jones, Elsie Clark, Beryl Kemp and Sheila Payton for help in
working up some of the garments and checking the instructions, and Enid Gomes for her help in
preparing the manuscript. Patchwork bricks on page 11 by Galt Toys Ltd., Prams on pages 34-35
by Mothercare; Dresses on pages 46-47 and 78-79 by Laura Ashley; Berets on pages 6 and 46 by
Kangol; Kilts on page 46 by John Lewis.

Photography and styling by Di Lewis
Line artwork by Lyn Savage

First published in 1980 by
The Hamlyn Publishing Group Limited
London · New York · Sydney · Toronto
Astronaut House, Feltham, Middlesex, England

Filmset in England by Photocomp Ltd, Birmingham
in 9 on 10pt. Rockwell Light

Printed in Singapore
ISBN 0 600 32068 5

Note: The photographs of the stitch details in the pattern
section are not necessarily actual size.

CONTENTS

INTRODUCTION

When I was writing this book I had novices at crochet very much in mind, especially those having to teach themselves as I did. There are, however, plenty of tips and designs which I am sure will be of interest even to the most experienced. All the basic stitches have been clearly described and illustrated for both the right handed and the left handed worker. Technical terms used in the written instructions are explained, tips on how to follow a pattern, achieve a professional finish and after-care have been included. There is even a 'Fault Chart'.

I have included a wide variety of patterns for babies, toddlers, teenagers and women and also household items to make from a vast range of different yarns. The majority are simple, requiring the minimum of fitting or intricate shaping, with the exception of the last few patterns which are for the more proficient. Some are quick to complete while others are larger and require more patience. Every design has something to teach, such as a new stitch, how to work a pocket or working different kinds of edgings. It is a good idea to work through the patterns in order of difficulty and practice every tension square even if you have no intention of actually producing the item itself, in this way a thorough grounding is basic crochet will be gained, I hope, with much pleasure.

HOW TO CROCHET FOR THE RIGHT HANDED

Full details and clear diagrams have been used to describe how to form all the crochet stitches in this book for both the right and left handed worker, so make sure you follow the ones which apply to you.

For your first attempt to crochet use a yarn of medium thickness: double knitting would be ideal, preferably with a creped finish. (Crepe is the particular way the yarn has been spun, it has extra twists and therefore is not so liable to split when worked). If double knitting is used then the correct hook would be a 4·50 mm (No. 7).

Practice the first stitch until it can be formed easily and evenly before advancing to the next and so on. Progressing slowly through all the stitches in this way will allow the crochet to flow and a rhythm to be maintained, which is essential for a good finish on the completed article.

Position of the hands

1 Position of the hook and right hand. The hook faces downwards at all times, thus allowing it to slip easily through the loops (Fig. 1).

2 Position of the left hand showing how the yarn is wound round the fingers. This is important for keeping the tension even throughout work (Fig. 2).

3 Position of both hands when working (Fig. 3).

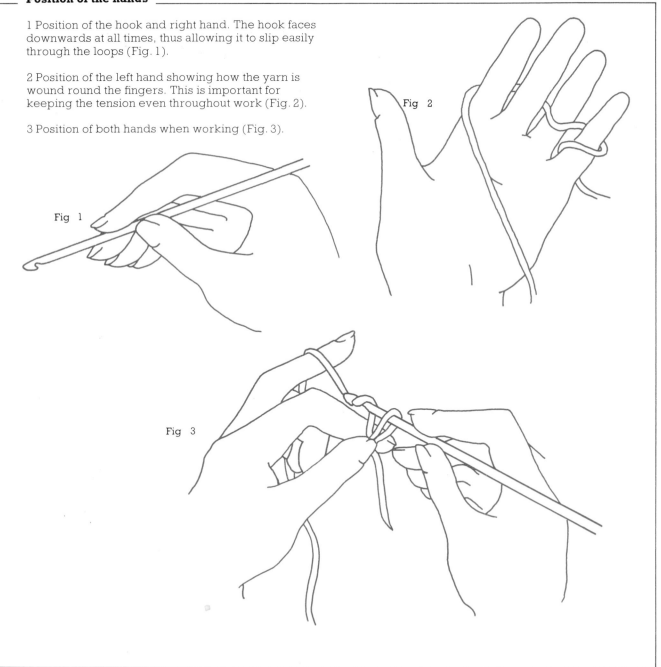

Fig 1

Fig 2

Fig 3

Slip Knot

Before crochet can begin an initial loop must be made and placed on to the hook. To make:– wind yarn once round first and second finger of left hand clockwise, insert hook into loop round fingers, yarn round hook and draw through. Leave loop on hook (Fig. 4).

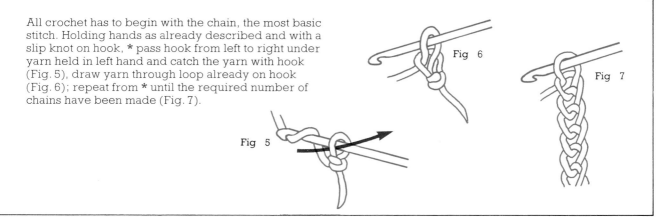

Fig 4

Chain (ch)

All crochet has to begin with the chain, the most basic stitch. Holding hands as already described and with a slip knot on hook, * pass hook from left to right under yarn held in left hand and catch the yarn with hook (Fig. 5), draw yarn through loop already on hook (Fig. 6); repeat from * until the required number of chains have been made (Fig. 7).

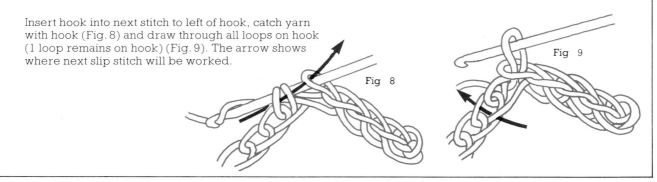

Fig 6

Fig 7

Fig 5

Slip Stitch (ss)

Insert hook into next stitch to left of hook, catch yarn with hook (Fig. 8) and draw through all loops on hook (1 loop remains on hook) (Fig. 9). The arrow shows where next slip stitch will be worked.

Fig 8

Fig 9

Double Crochet (dc)

Insert hook into next stitch to left of hook, catch yarn with hook (Fig. 10), draw yarn through stitch (2 loops on hook), yarn over hook (Fig. 11) and draw yarn through both loops on hook (1 loop remains on hook) (Fig. 12). Arrow in (Fig. 12) shows where next double crochet will be worked.

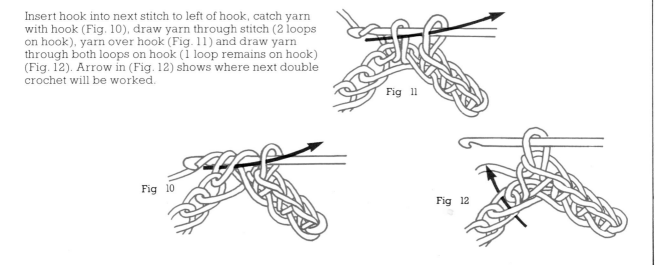

Fig 11

Fig 10

Fig 12

Half Treble (hlf tr)

Pass yarn over hook (Fig. 13), insert hook into next stitch to left of hook, catch yarn with hook and draw through first 2 loops on hook, yarn over hook (Fig. 14) and draw through all 3 loops on hook (1 loop remains on hook) (Fig. 15). Arrow in (Fig. 15) shows where next half treble will be worked.

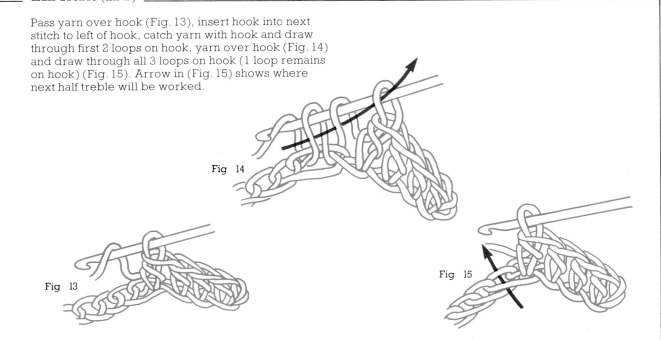

Fig 14

Fig 13

Fig 15

Treble (tr)

Pass yarn over hook (Fig. 16), insert hook into next stitch to left of hook, catch yarn with hook and draw a loop through first 2 loops on hook, yarn over hook (Fig. 17) and draw through next 2 loops on hook, yarn over hook (Fig. 18) and draw through 2 remaining loops (1 loop remains on hook) (Fig. 19). Arrow in (Fig. 19) shows where next treble will be worked.

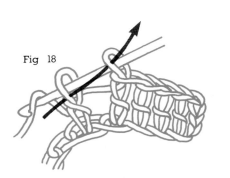

Fig 18

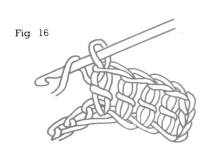

Fig 16

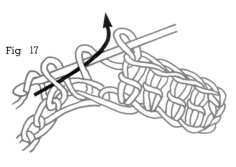

Fig 17

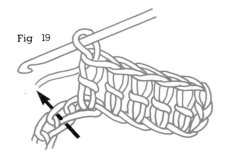

Fig 19

Double Treble (dbl tr)

Pass yarn over hook twice (Fig. 20), insert hook into next stitch to left of hook, catch yarn with hook and draw through first 2 loops on hook (4 loops remain on hook), yarn over hook (Fig. 21) and draw through next 2 loops on hook (3 loops remain on hook), yarn over hook (Fig. 22) and draw through next 2 loops on hook (2 loops remain on hook, yarn over hook (Fig. 23) and draw through 2 remaining loops (1 loop remains on hook) (Fig. 24). Arrow in (Fig. 24) shows where next double treble will be worked.

It can be seen from the diagrams of the treble and double treble that they are formed in the same way except that the latter has been made longer by winding the yarn round the hook one extra time at the commencement of the stitch. The yarn has been wound round the hook once for the treble (Fig. 16) and twice for the double treble (Fig. 20). Stitches longer than the double treble can be made, the next would have the yarn wound round the hook 3 times at the commencement and be called a triple treble. The next would have the yarn wound round 4 times and be called a quadruple treble. There is no limit to how many more stitches can be made in this way, each one longer than the previous but none have been described here because they have not been used for any of the designs in this book.

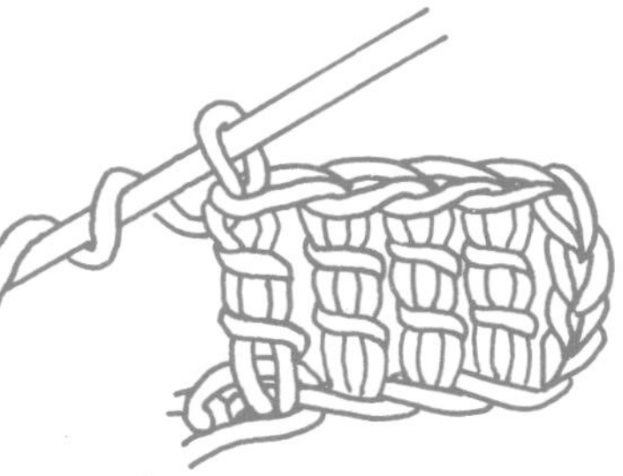

Fig 20

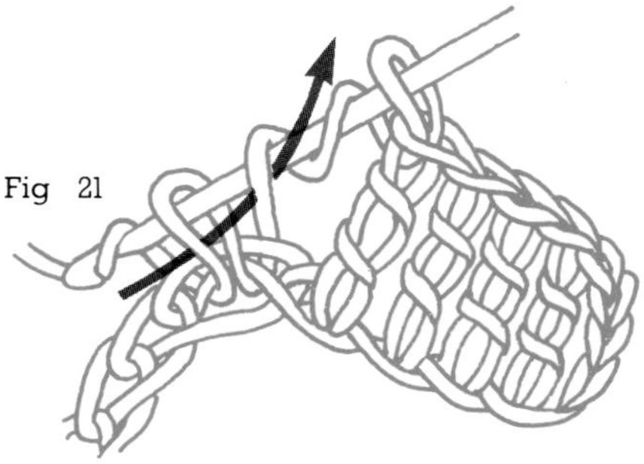

Fig 21

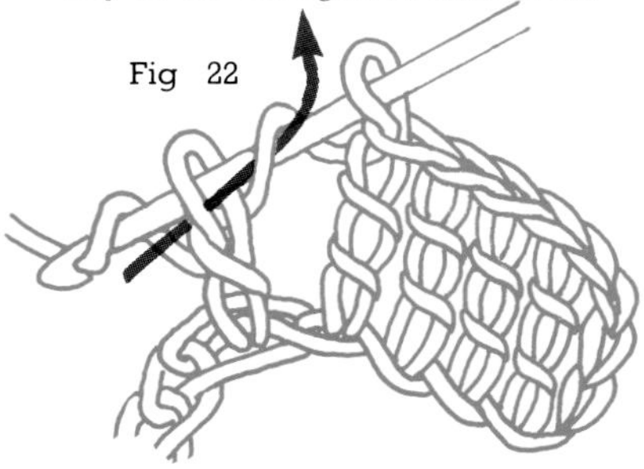

Fig 22

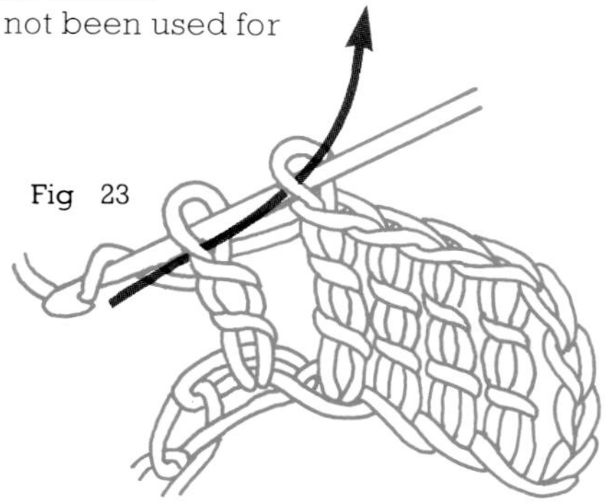

Fig 23

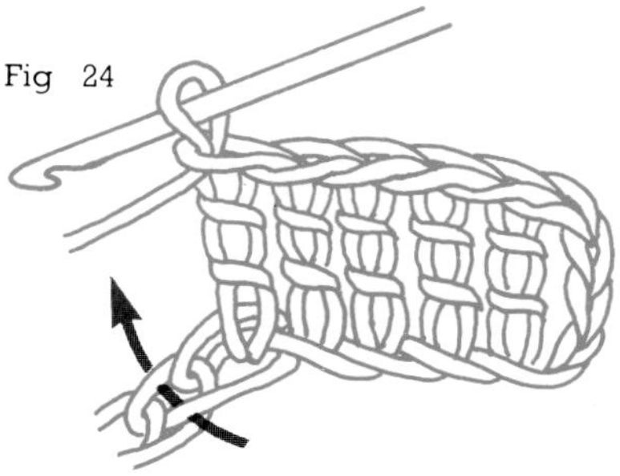

Fig 24

Grouped Stitches

The stitches here are made from groups of the basic stitches or from groups of parts of the basic stitches. The diagrams show how the stitches have been worked for the designs in this book. These grouped stitches can be made with more or less stitches, thus making them thicker or thinner, so, although the groups may look similar, it is important to work them as the particular instructions describe otherwise the fabric will come out too wide or too narrow.

Picot
Make 3 chain (Fig. 25), insert hook into front loop and side loop of last stitch made before the 3 chain (the arrow in Fig. 25 shows these 2 loops), yarn over hook and draw through all 3 loops on hook (Fig. 26).

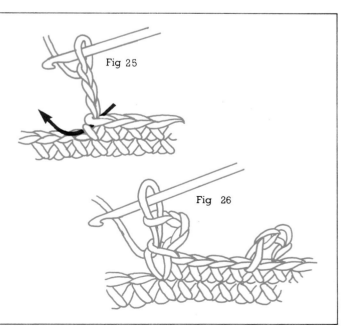

Fig 25

Fig 26

Cluster

Pass yarn over hook, * insert hook into appropriate stitch to left of hook, yarn over hook and draw through first 2 loops on hook, yarn over hook and draw through next 2 loops on hook, yarn over hook (Fig. 27); rep. from * 3 times more into same place (Fig. 28) end by drawing last loop through all 5 loops on hook.

Clusters can also be made with each treble worked into a different stitch which gives a triangle shaped group.

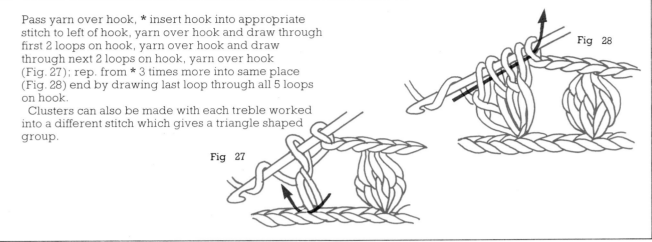

Puff Stitch (puff st)

* Pass yarn over hook, insert hook into appropriate stitch to left of hook, yarn over hook and draw a loop up to the same height as work (Fig. 29); rep from * 3 times more into same place, end with yarn over hook (Fig. 30), draw loop through all 9 loops on hook.

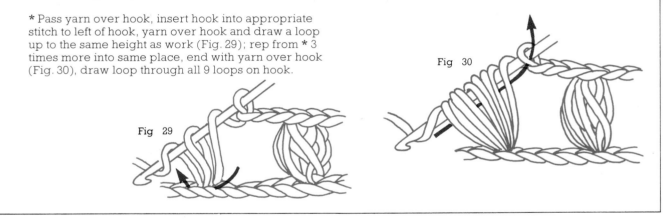

Bullion Stitch (bullion st)

Pass yarn over hook 9 times, insert hook into appropriate stitch to left of hook, yarn over hook and draw a loop through, yarn over hook (Fig. 31) and draw through all 11 loops on hook.

The bullion stitch gives a beautiful texture but is quite difficult to work. The knack is to keep the yarn loose and even as it is wound 9 times round the hook so that when the loop and hook are pulled through all the threads they do not get caught up. If difficulty is still experienced then substitute a puff stitch in its place.

Popcorn

Work 4 trebles all into appropriate stitch, remove hook from loop, insert hook into top of first treble (picking up 2 stitches), catch the dropped loop (Fig. 32) and draw it through both loops on hook, secure with 1 chain.

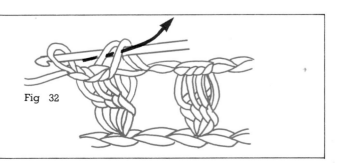

Shell

Work 6 trebles into one stitch (Fig. 33). This is described as a 6 treble shell. Shells of 4 and 5 trebles are also used in this book.

Fig 33

Beaded Treble (beaded tr)

Before beginning the stitch thread some beads on to yarn. Pass yarn over hook, insert hook into appropriate stitch and draw a loop through, yarn over hook and draw through first 2 loops, drop 2 beads down behind work, yarn over hook (Fig. 34) and draw through both remaining loops on hook.

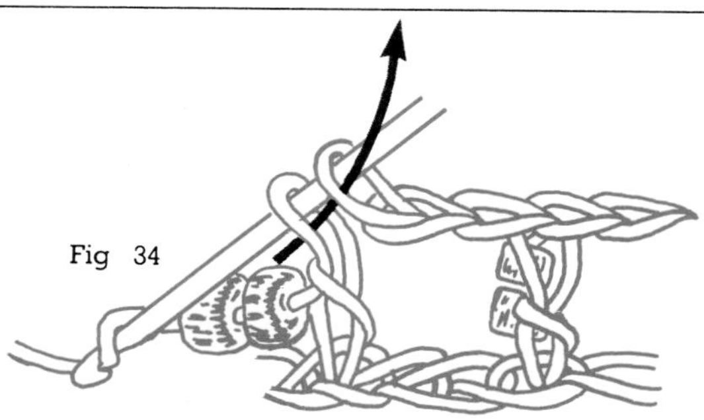

Fig 34

Joining a Ring for Motifs

Make a chain of 6 stitches. Join together by inserting hook into first chain made, yarn over hook (Fig. 35) and draw through all loops on hook.

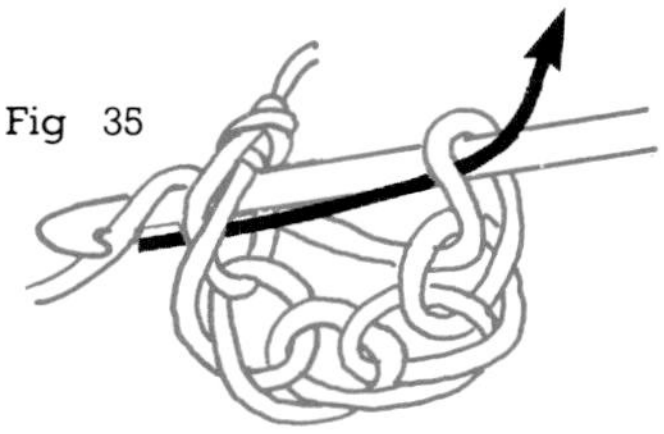

Fig 35

Loop Stitch

Pass yarn over middle finger and under first finger of left hand loosely, insert hook into next stitch to left of work, catch yarn with hook (Fig. 36) and draw a loop through first 2 loops on hook, yarn over hook (Fig. 37) and draw through remaining 2 loops on hook (1 loop remains on hook). Remove loop from finger, this will fall to the back of row being worked.
   Take care that all subsequent loops made around finger are of similar length.

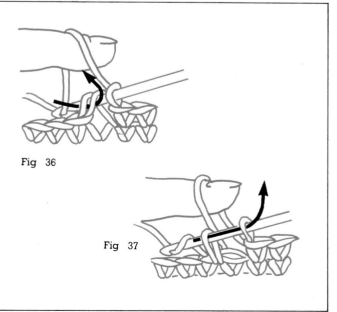

Fig 36

Fig 37

HOW TO CROCHET FOR THE LEFT HANDED

The comment 'I can't crochet because I'm left handed' is frequently heard. This is nonsense, of course. A person who can knit right handed will find it especially easy to crochet left handed because the hands are held in the same position and the yarn wrapped around the same hand (the right one) as for knitting.

Follow the instructions as written, there is no need to read pattern rows from end to beginning, just remember that because the crochet is being worked the opposite way the word 'right' will always turn out 'left' and vice versa. Alter these two words in the instructions every time they appear, so that what was originally described as a right front will now be a left front and so on. Label each piece as it is made, then there will be no confusion at the making up stage.

Buttonholes are the only thing that will need complete alteration because they will end up on the opposite side of the design if the instructions are followed as written. You will have to work them on the side they are needed, otherwise a cardigan intended for a girl could end up as a boy's cardigan.

All the diagrams in this section are drawn to show the method of working for a left-handed person. The diagrams throughout the rest of the book are right-handed, to transpose these with ease hold the book up to a mirror and follow the diagram in the reflection.

Position of the Hands

1 Fig. 38 shows the position of the hook and left hand: the hook faces downwards at all times, thus allowing it to slip easily through the loops.

2 Position of the right hand showing how the yarn is wound round the fingers (Fig. 39). This is important for keeping the tension even throughout work.

3 Position of both hands when working (Fig. 40).

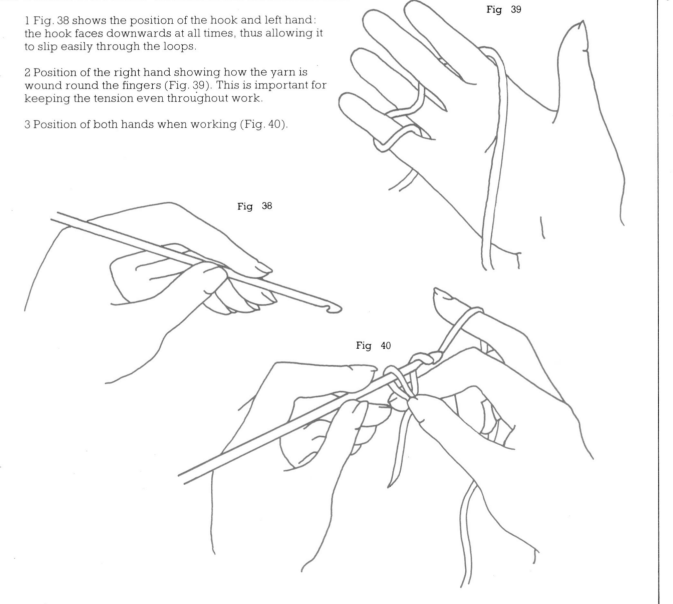

Fig 39

Fig 38

Fig 40

Basic Stitches (in order of height)

Slip Knot

Before crochet can begin an initial loop must be made and placed on to the hook. To make:– wind yarn once round first and second fingers of right hand anti-clockwise, insert hook into loop round fingers, wind yarn round hook and draw through. Leave loop on hook (Fig. 41).

Fig 41

Chain (ch)

All crochet has to begin with the chain, the most basic stitch. Holding hands as already described and with a slip knot on hook, * pass hook from right to left under yarn held in right hand and catch the yarn with hook (Fig. 42), draw yarn through loop already on hook (Fig. 43); repeat from * until the required number of chains have been made (Fig. 44).

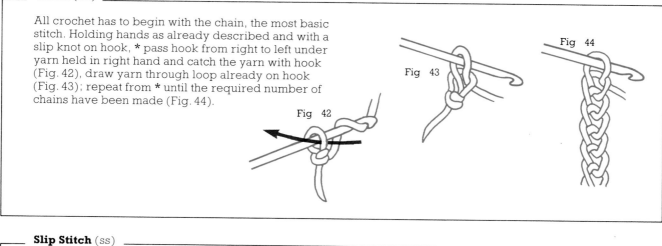

Fig 44

Fig 43

Fig 42

Slip Stitch (ss)

Insert hook into next stitch to right of hook, catch yarn with hook (Fig. 45) and draw through all loops on hook (1 loop remains on hook) (Fig. 46). Arrow in (Fig. 46) shows where next slip stitch will be worked.

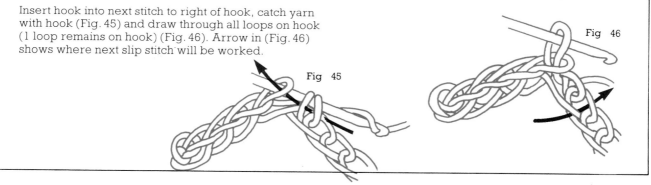

Fig 46

Fig 45

Double Crochet (dc)

Insert hook into next stitch to right of hook, catch yarn with hook (Fig. 47), draw yarn through stitch (2 loops on hook), yarn over hook (Fig. 48) and draw yarn through both loops on hook (1 loop remains on hook) (Fig. 49). Arrow in (Fig. 49) shows where next double crochet will be worked.

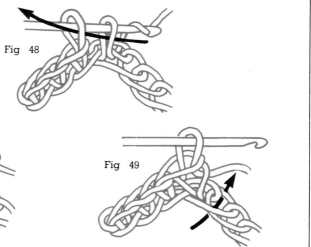

Fig 48

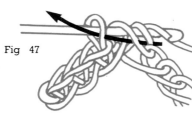

Fig 47

Fig 49

Half Treble (hlf tr)

Pass yarn over hook (Fig. 50), insert hook into next stitch to right of hook, catch yarn with hook and draw through first 2 loops on hook, yarn over hook (Fig. 51) and draw through all 3 loops on hook (1 loop remains on hook) (Fig. 52). Arrow in (Fig. 52) shows where next half treble will be worked.

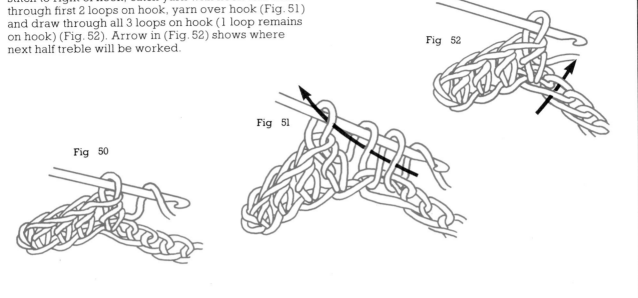

Fig 52

Fig 51

Fig 50

Treble (tr)

Pass yarn over hook (Fig. 53), insert hook into next stitch to right of hook, catch yarn with hook and draw a loop through first 2 loops on hook, yarn over hook (Fig. 54) and draw through next 2 loops on hook, yarn over hook (Fig. 55) and draw through 2 remaining loops (1 loop remains on hook) (Fig. 56). Arrow in (Fig. 56) shows where next treble will be worked.

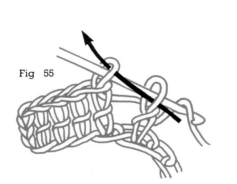

Fig 55

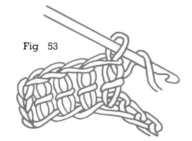

Fig 53

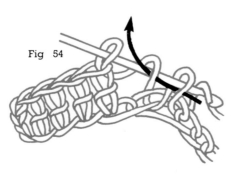

Fig 54

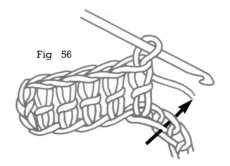

Fig 56

Double Treble (dbl tr)

Pass yarn over hook twice (Fig. 57), insert hook into next stitch to right of hook, catch yarn with hook and draw through first 2 loops on hook (4 loops remain on hook), yarn over hook (Fig. 58) and draw through next 2 loops on hook (3 loops remain on hook), yarn over hook (Fig. 59) and draw through next 2 loops on hook (2 loops remain on hook, yarn over hook (Fig. 60) and draw through 2 remaining loops (1 loop remains on hook) (Fig. 61). Arrow in (Fig. 61) shows where next double treble will be worked.

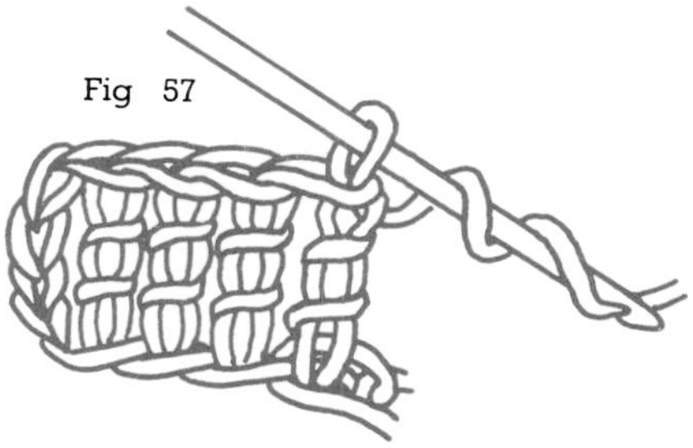

It can be seen from the diagrams of the treble and double treble that they are formed in the same way except that the latter has been made longer by winding the yarn round the hook one extra time at the commencement of the stitch. The yarn has been wound round the hook once for the treble (Fig. 53) and twice for the double treble (Fig. 57). Stitches longer than the double treble can be made, the next would have the yarn wound round the hook 3 times at the start of the stitch and be called a triple treble. The next would have the yarn wound round 4 times and be called a quadruple treble. There is no limit to how many more stitches can be made in this way, each one longer than the previous but none have been described here because they have not been used for any of the designs in this book.

Fig 57

Fig 58

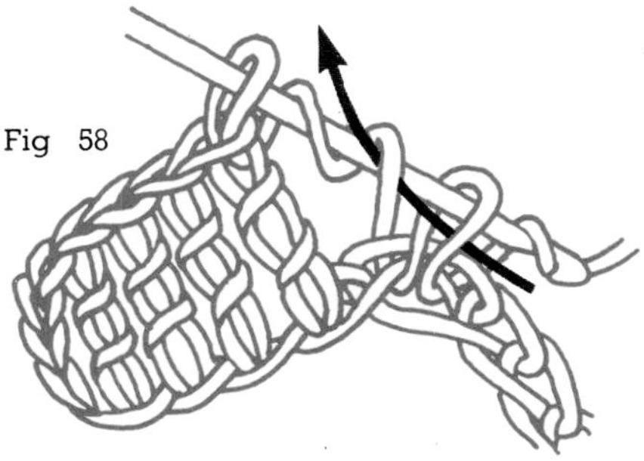

Fig 59

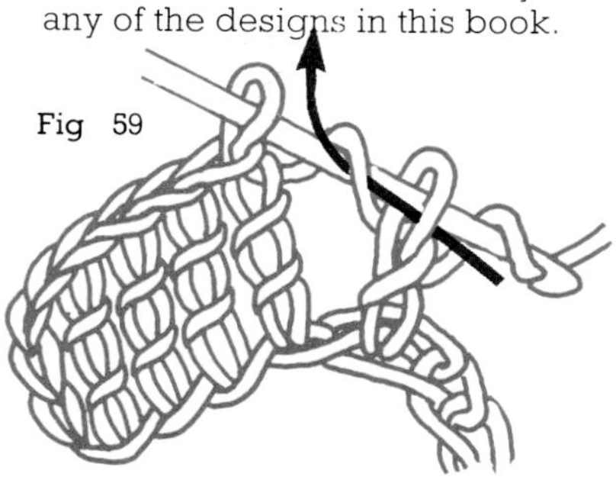

Fig 60

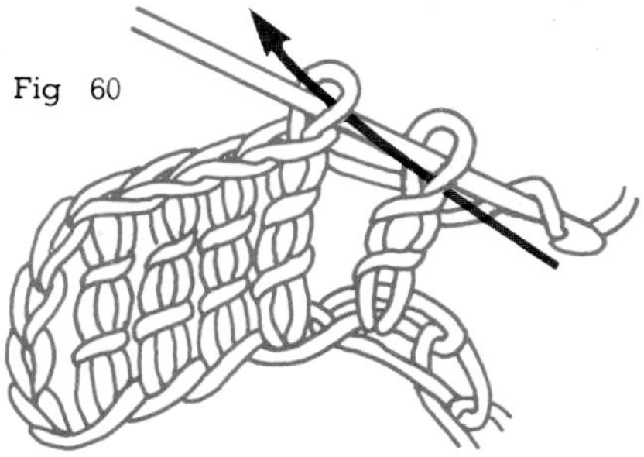

Fig 61

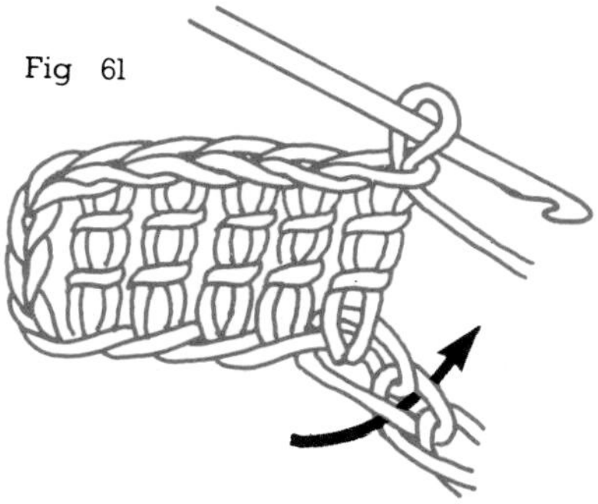

Grouped Stitches

The stitches here are made from groups of the basic stitches or from groups of parts of the basic stitches. The diagrams show how the stitches have been worked for the designs in this book. These grouped stitches can be made with more or less stitches thus making them thicker and thinner, so, although the groups may look similar it is important to work them as the particular instructions describe otherwise the fabric will come out too wide or too narrow.

Picot

Make 3 chain (Fig. 62), insert hook into front loop and side loop of last stitch made before the 3 chain; the arrow in Fig. 62 shows these 2 loops. Yarn over hook and draw through all 3 loops on hook (Fig. 63).

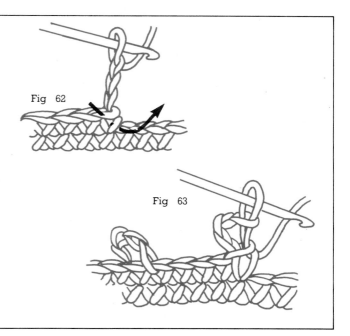

Fig 62

Fig 63

Cluster

Pass yarn over hook, * insert hook into appropriate stitch to right of hook, yarn over hook and draw through first 2 loops on hook, yarn over hook and draw through next 2 loops on hook, yarn over hook (Fig. 64); repeat from * 3 times more into same place (Fig. 65), end by drawing last loop through all 5 loops on hook.

Clusters can also be made with each treble worked into a different stitch which gives a triangular shaped group.

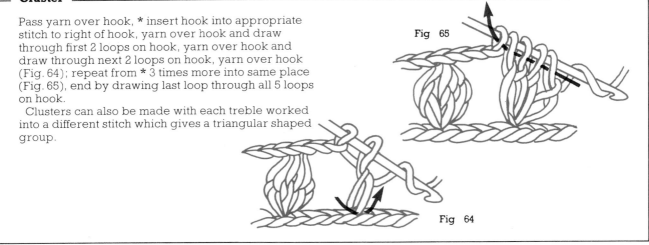

Fig 65

Fig 64

Puff Stitch (puff st)

* Pass yarn over hook, insert hook into appropriate stitch to right of hook, yarn over hook and draw a loop up to the same height as work (Fig. 66); repeat from * 3 times more into same place, end with yarn over hook (Fig. 67), draw loop through all 9 loops on hook.

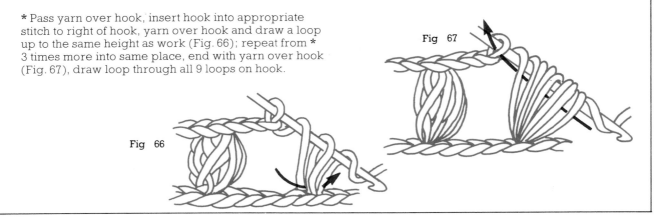

Fig 67

Fig 66

Bullion Stitch (bullion st)

Pass yarn over hook 9 times, insert hook into appropriate stitch to right of hook, yarn over hook and draw a loop through, yarn over hook (Fig. 68) and draw through all 11 loops on hook.

The bullion stitch gives a beautiful texture but is quite difficult to work. The knack is to keep the yarn loose and even as it is wound 9 times round the hook so that when the loop and hook are pulled through all the threads they do not get caught up. If difficulty is still experienced then substitute a puff stitch in its place.

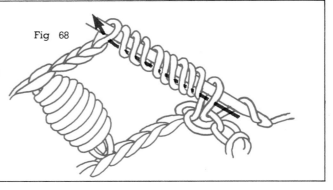

Fig 68

Popcorn

Work 4 trebles all into appropriate stitch, remove hook from loop, insert hook into top of first treble (picking up 2 stitches), catch the dropped loop (Fig. 69) and draw it through both loops on hook, secure with 1 chain.

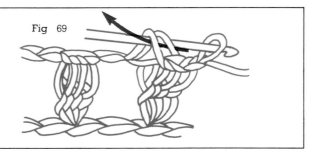

Fig 69

Shell

Work 6 trebles into one stitch (Fig. 70). This is described as a 6 treble shell. Shells of 4 and 5 trebles are also used in this book.

Fig 70

Beaded Treble (beaded tr)

Before beginning thread some beads on to yarn. Pass yarn over hook, insert hook into appropriate stitch and draw a loop through, yarn over hook and draw through first 2 loops, drop 2 beads down behind work, yarn over hook (Fig. 71) and draw through both remaining loops on hook.

Fig 71

Joining a Ring for Motifs

Make a chain of 6 stitches. Join together by inserting hook into first chain made, yarn over hook (Fig. 72) and draw through all loops on hook.

Fig 72

Loop Stitch

Pass yarn over middle finger and under first finger of right hand loosely, insert hook into next stitch to right of work, catch yarn with hook (Fig. 73) and draw a loop through first 2 loops on hook, yarn over hook (Fig. 74) and draw through remaining 2 loops on hook (1 loop remains on hook). Remove loop from finger, this will fall to the back of row being worked.

Take care that all subsequent loops made around finger are of similar length.

Fig 73

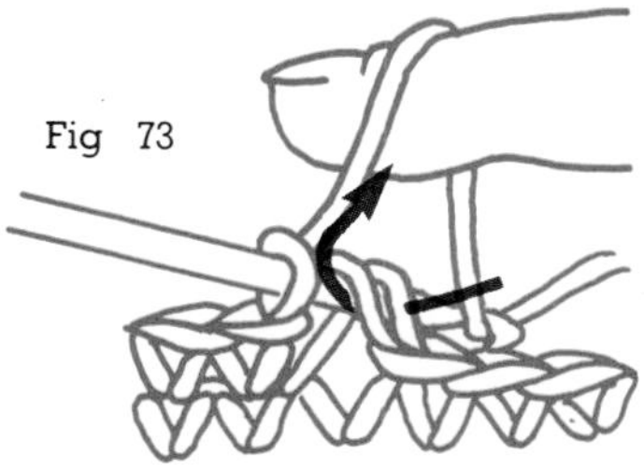

Fig 74

HELPFUL INFORMATION

Having learned the crochet stitches read through this chapter before attempting to crochet your first item. Here technical terms are explained and common pitfalls are pointed out to help you follow written instructions correctly.

Choosing the Pattern

To begin with make simple things like shawls, hats and scarves. These items do not require precise fitting so that if the tension is not quite correct the results are not disastrous. Make sure the instructions are printed clearly and, if possible, there is a close-up photograph included of the stitch pattern used. The latter can be most helpful: many a time when I was learning I had to follow the picture because I did not understand the instructions. Patterns are usually quite lengthy because every step is explained in full. You will find in this book that all the shapings are written in full, every stitch is described and where it is to be worked is mentioned. Nothing has been left for you to work out.

Keeping Work Clean

Make sure that hands are clean and dry at all times. Dirty marks in the actual yarn should not be used, cut them out. Never allow the ball of yarn to roll around an unclean floor or allow hair to get caught in the work. Be careful with delicate shades, use yarn from the centre of the ball that has been placed in a large paper bag, keep the bag in position with a loose elastic band round its neck thus preventing the ball from popping out. The finished end of a large section still being worked should be protected by tying a cloth around. Keep all crochet wrapped when not actually working on it. All these precautions will help to avoid soiling.

The Materials

The Yarn

The word 'yarn' has been used throughout this book to describe both natural and man-made fibres. Always buy sufficient of the specified yarn to complete the article as dye lots vary. Yarns differ in thickness, texture and elasticity, therefore, if another is substituted for the one quoted then the article may take more yarn, stretch with use or end up the wrong size.

Avoid loosely spun yarn until you are proficient as it is apt to split. Begin with crepes and those tightly twisted.

Mohairs, brushed acrylics and tweedy yarns are quite simple to use after a little practice. When using these yarns make sure that each part of every stitch is pulled up so as to allow the hairs or lumps to come through the loops. This will prevent the length tension being too short, the stitches looking squat, the texture feeling hard and avoid difficulty in actually working with the yarn. All these problems can be caused because the loop around the hook is being kept exceptionally tight. If the work can be pulled undone easily then the loops are large enough and the tension is correct.

Other Items

Have any other required item to hand but never purchase buttons until the buttonholes have been worked. Buy the buttons to fit the buttonholes and so avoid using the wrong size. Buttons which continually come undone are only a source of annoyance.

The Hook

Start with the quoted hook size, altering this only if the tension is incorrect. Choose crochet hooks carefully when buying them, the more rounded the hook part the better. Sharp ones (a common fault with those of bone) and those too small for the thickness of yarn will tend to split the loops.

Understanding the Pattern

Sizes

Throughout this book the figures in square brackets e.g. [ ] refer to larger sizes, where only one figure is given this refers to all sizes. To avoid confusion underline those which refer to your particular size.

Metrication

All measurements are given in metric quantities, 'mm' 'cm' etc., followed by imperial measurements in brackets. Crochet hook sizes are given in the same way with the metric measurement in mm followed by the English size. There may be slight variations when comparing metric with imperial because they have been taken to the nearest 0·5 cm or to the nearest ¼ in. The important point to remember is to work entirely according to one set of measurements. Never switch from metric to imperial half way through the pattern or vice versa.

Which Size?

First take the following measurements:– the chest all round at the widest part below underarm (Fig. 75) A; the length from the highest point of shoulder, B; and the length of sleeve from below underarm to wrist, C. Do not pull the tape-measure too tight and do not use one made from woven fabric as they are apt to stretch.

Follow instructions for the same size as the chest measurement, for example, if the chest measured 86 cm (34 in) all round then follow the instructions for size 86 cm (34 in). A movement allowance has already been made on all garments in this book (Fig. 76) D, will be half the chest and movement allowance.

Where to Adjust the Length

When the quoted length of sleeve is not required alter the length at the underarm just before the crown shaping (Fig. 76) E. Alter the length from shoulder at underarm just before armhole shaping (Fig. 76) F.

Measuring the Length

The weight of the yarn will always pull the garment down when it is being worn, counteract this when taking any length measurement by holding work and tape-measure up. Quite a difference will be made on the length of an armhole using this method for example; these should never be too large otherwise the sleeves cannot be set in properly.

When the design to be made is worked from the waist or underarm upwards, then stitches picked up

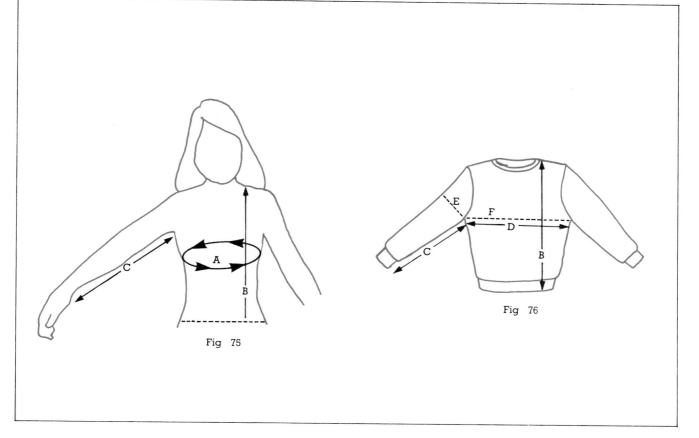

Fig 75

Fig 76

along the commencing chain and worked down, crochet a few rows of the bodice only, make the lower section next and finally return to complete the bodice. This again allows the weight of the yarn to effect the length measurements.

Instructions sometimes require you to end on a certain pattern row when work is a particular length, if this is impossible make the length shorter rather than longer but always finish with the correct row.

Tension

Two factors affect tension: the thickness of the crochet hook and the tightness of the yarn wound around the fingers. It is the latter which causes beginners to work too tightly or to vary erratically. An even flow of yarn is essential for neat work and only practice will achieve this.

Tension must be checked every time a different article is to be made, no one can crochet so well that this is unnecessary. Tension is quoted at the beginning of every pattern and as it is from this that the instructions have been written. Your tension must be the same in order to produce an item the quoted size. How to make a tension sample has been fully described for every design in this book so spare a few moments and make it.

How to Check your Tension

Work the tension square quoted using the correct yarn and hook. Fasten off. Lay the square down on a flat surface.

Width Without stretching the square measure the width. If the width is smaller than that quoted then use

a size larger hook, if larger then use a size smaller hook. Work another square and check again.

Length Once the width tension is correct and if a length tension has also been quoted this must now be checked. This is essential when anything worked in rounds is being made otherwise the article will not lie correctly but will cockle round the edge. If the length is smaller then it will be necessary to pull up every stitch slightly more than usual, if longer then do not pull the stitches up so much.

Abbreviations

The abbreviations used in this book are as follows:—

ch – chain;	sp – space;
ss – slip stitch;	lp(s) – loop(s);
dc – double crochet;	rep – repeat;
hlf tr – half treble;	patt – pattern;
tr – treble;	in – inch(es);
dbl tr – double treble;	cm – centimetre(s);
M – main colour;	DK – double knitting;
C – contrast;	g – grams;
1 st C – 1 st contrast;	dec – decrease;
2nd C – 2nd contrast;	Fig(s) – figure(s);
st(s) – stitch(es);	
No – number;	
inc – increase;	
mm – millimetre(s);	

∗ – Asterisk. Repeat instructions following the asterisk as many times as specified in addition to the original.

( ) – brackets. Repeat instructions in brackets as many times as specified. For example '(1 tr into next ch, 1 ch) 4 times' means work everything in ( ) 4 times altogether.

How to Begin

To make the initial loop start with a slip knot, for the right-handed refer to Fig. 4 on page 13 and for the left-handed refer to Fig. 41 on page 19. Make certain that the loop can be pulled tight afterwards to avoid a hole forming in the work and that the end left hanging is of a reasonable length. Motif centres in particular take a great deal of strain and are apt to loosen once the article is in use, so thread a needle with the loose end of the yarn and oversew securely before darning in. All loose ends must be securely fastened.

Sometimes, when working motifs, the instructions require the yarn to be wrapped around finger a number of times to form a ring (Fig. 77), these loops are not meant to be pulled up but are used to make an extra thick beginning circle when a round of double crochet is worked. Fig. 78 shows the ring removed from the finger and Fig. 79 shows double crochets actually being worked.

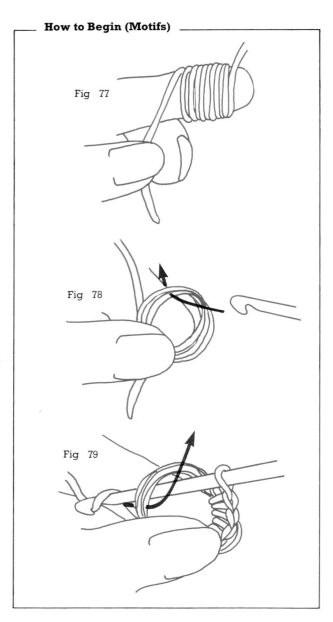

How to Begin (Motifs)

Fig 77

Fig 78

Fig 79

The Commencing Chain

All crochet begins with a length of chain (see the section on basic stitches), it is important that this foundation chain is the correct length and is worked evenly otherwise the beginning edge of the work will cockle. The required length of the commencing chain is quoted in every design throughout this book. Measure it lying flat, being careful not to stretch it. If the chain length continually comes up too small, work it on a larger hook then return to the normal hook for the next row.

Never count the loop on the hook when counting the number of chains made. This applies throughout.

Rows and Rounds

The word 'row' is used to denote that lines of stitches are worked back and forth across the crochet turning at the end of every row to keep the continuity of the thread.

Working in 'rounds' is common for edgings and motifs when the rows of stitches are worked continuously round. The end of a round has to be joined up to its beginning, usually with a slip stitch, to complete the circle. There is no need to turn unless told to do so. If difficulty is experienced distinguishing the beginning of a round from the rest of the work then use a coloured thread to mark the first stitch of a new round as soon as it is made.

'Working in continuous rounds' is a common phrase used when several rounds of double crochets are to be made. Because the length of a double crochet is quite short it is possible to start the next round with a double crochet into the first double crochet of the previous round without first joining the loose end of the previous round into its beginning. Mark the end of each round with a coloured thread as it is quite easy to work more than the required amount. End the last round with a slip stitch worked into the next double crochet.

The Foundation Row

The foundation row is always worked into the commencing chain. For a firm beginning always pick up 2 loops when working any stitch into this chain (refer to all the diagrams of the basic stitches).

Working the Next Rows

All stitches should be worked into the two top loops of every stitch throughout the work, unless the instructions say 'working into back loops only' or 'working into front loops only'. Diagrams here show a double crochet being worked into a double crochet on the previous row in the normal way (Fig. 80), a double crochet being worked into the front loop only (Fig. 81) and a double crochet being worked into the back loop only (Fig. 82).

The Turning Chain

To allow the hook to be at the correct height ready for the next row, chains are worked. These are referred to as 'turning chains', B in Fig. 83. The number of chains to be made varies according to the length of stitch to be worked along the row. Be careful to work the correct number otherwise the sides will cockle:

double crochet – 1 chain (sometimes 0)
half treble   – 2 chains
treble   – 3 chains
double treble – 4 chains

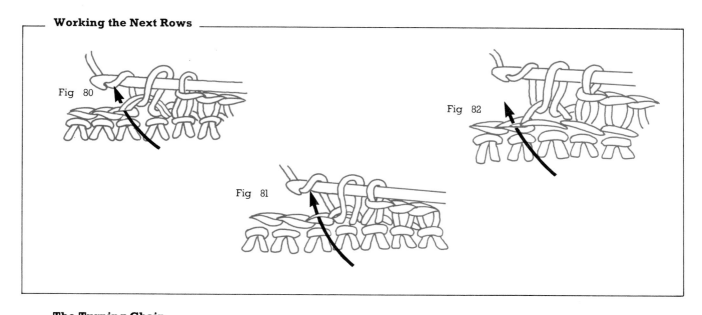

Fig 80

Fig 81

Fig 82

The Turning Chain

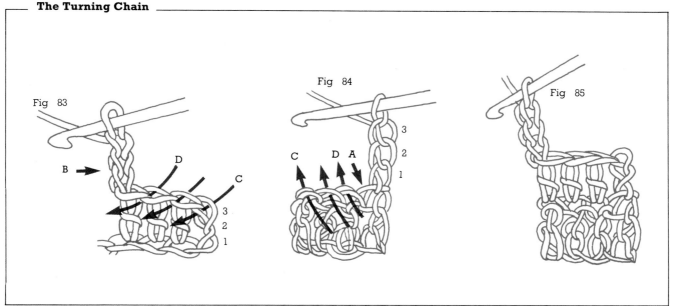

Fig 83

B

D

C

3
2
1

Fig 84

C

D A

3
2
1

Fig 85

Figs. 83 and 84 show trebles being worked, Fig. 83 before the work is turned and Fig. 84 after the work is turned ready to continue.

This 'turning chain' counts as the first stitch of the row, this is why instructions say 'miss first stitch' when a straight piece is being crocheted. A in Fig. 84 marks the stitch to be missed and D in both cases marks the next stitch to be worked into.

The last stitch of the row has to be worked into the top chain of the 'turning chain' standing for the first stitch of the previous row, C in Figs. 83 and 84. The actual chain to be worked into is named, in our diagram example the instructions would say '1 tr into 3 rd of 3 ch'. These chains are always counted from the bottom up, marked 1, 2 and 3 in Fig. 83. Be sure to work into the correct one otherwise the side of the crochet will cockle. The row completed is shown in Fig. 85.

When counting the number of stitches completed in a row, the 'turning chain' counts only as one stitch.

Counting Stitches

It is easy, especially when just learning to crochet, to have the wrong number of stitches, so, in this book a stitch total has been quoted at the end of foundation rows and important or difficult shaping rows. Check that you have the same number of stitches as that quoted before proceeding.

The most common error to watch for is unintentionally increasing at the beginning of rows and decreasing at the ends, resulting in sloping sides to the crochet.

Remember, once again, the 'turning chain' counts as one stitch.

Counting Rows

Make certain that similar pieces of work such as sleeves and front pieces have the same number of rows; crochet stitches tend to be rather long so 1 row difference between a right and left front for example can make 1 cm (½ in) difference.

Spaces and Loops

The difference between a space (Fig. 86) and a loop (Fig. 87) is visual only. When a stitch has to be worked into either, the hook is inserted through the gap and then the yarn pulled through. For clarity particular spaces and loops are referred to in this book by their number of chains wherever possible, for example a '6 ch sp', a '4 ch lp'.

Working Round Trebles

Interesting textures similar to a knitted rib or a basket weave effect can be achieved by working the trebles round the ones on the row below. There are two methods, either the stitch lies at the front of the work (Fig. 88) or at the back (Fig. 89). When 'working round back of treble' (Fig. 88), the hook is inserted round the treble from front to back and out the other side, the yarn is then picked up and pulled round. When 'working round front of treble' (Fig. 89), the hook is inserted round the treble from the back to front and out the other side, the yarn is picked up and pulled round.

Joining on New Yarn

Always join new yarn at the beginning of a row. Never join in the middle and try to work over the 2 ends, this will result in a weaker join and an unsightly bulge will probably appear.

Increasing and Decreasing

Any increasing or decreasing is described in full throughout this book. When decreasing across the top of a row described as '1 ss into each of next x sts', never work a slip stitch into the very first stitch of the previous row. Make sure that the slip stitches are worked loosely and do not mis-shape the crochet. When told to 'ss to centre of next shell', work a slip stitch loosely into every stitch until the centre space of the required shell is reached.

Multicolour Work

Working in more than one colour can be very complicated so this book will only cover the most simple multicolour work, that is where whole rows are worked in single-coloured stripes. There are no colour changes within the rows.

The problems of multicolour work arise not in the actual working of the stitches but at the edges of the work where the various colours are left hanging. An easy answer would be to fasten off the colours as they have been used but this results in lots of ends to darn in and is not really very satisfactory. Instructions in this book say when to join a new colour, turn and fasten off. Do not do any of these things unless told, otherwise rows could be inside out.

Example Work 1 row in the specified colour (light in Figs. 90 and 91), leave the yarn hanging at the end of the row, do not fasten off (Fig. 90). Work the next row in the required colour (dark in Fig. 91) making sure that the last loop formed at the end of the previous row is caught, thus preventing that row from unravelling. The arrow in Fig. 90 shows where to insert the hook. When the first colour is needed again just loop it up to the required row loosely (A in Fig. 91) and work in the usual manner. Loops of coloured yarn will be left at the edges of the work, leave them there, when the article is made up keep them on the reverse side or work an edging over them. Do not leave long loops

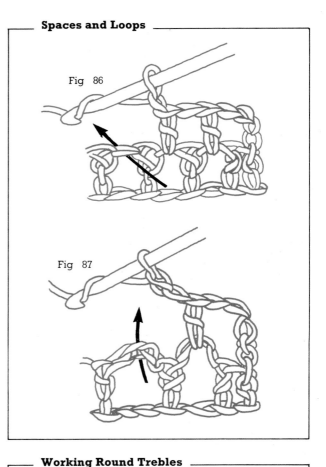

Spaces and Loops

Fig 86

Fig 87

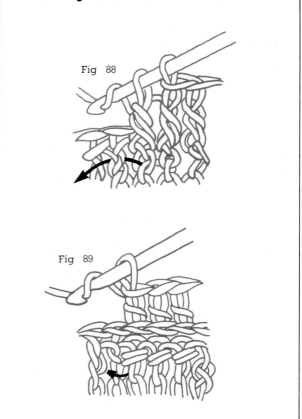

Working Round Trebles

Fig 88

Fig 89

as they are apt to catch, allow enough yarn only to lie flat against the side edge.

It can also be seen from the example that it is not necessary to turn work after every row, in Fig. 91 it will be turned only at the end of every alternate row. Two rows will face one way and then two rows the opposite way throughout.

Bead Work

The effect of using beads in crochet can be very attractive. They are normally used on trebles (see basic stitches page 14 (right-handed) and 20 (left-handed). The beads always fall to the back of the stitch therefore the reverse side when working will be used as the right side of the fabric. Use only beads with large holes, commonly known as knitting beads. To help thread them on to the yarn use thin fuse wire which is much finer than a needle. Take a length of wire 8 cm (3 in) long, fold in half, loop it round the yarn and twist the two ends together twice. Thread both ends through each bead (Fig. 92).

The bead centres are usually dirty, especially glass ones which are full of sand, so, when the required number have been threaded on, push them up the yarn several times until they are clean. Cut off the soiled yarn; do not crochet with it. Beads cannot be slipped on to a second thread, they have to be threaded again, so to avoid this, make sure there is plenty of yarn in the ball and check that it is free of knots and lumps.

Right Side of Work

Quite a number of crochet stitch patterns are reversible, it is therefore for you to decide which will be the right side. Make sure all the pieces are the same way up and mark them, thus avoiding the mistake of joining sleeves or fronts inside out.

Work motifs with right sides facing throughout unless the instructions say 'turn'. Be careful when joining motifs together that they all are facing upwards, it is very easy to join one upside down.

Multicolour Work

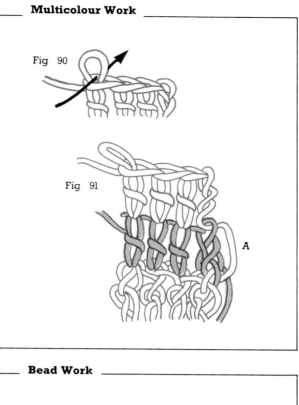

Fig 90

Fig 91

A

Bead Work

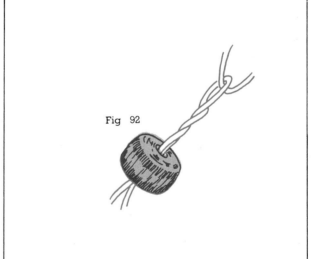

Fig 92

PROFESSIONAL FINISHING TOUCHES

A little extra time taken at the finishing stage of any article can achieve wonders. Here are some helpful hints.

Darning in Ends
Once each section has been made secure darn in ends with a tapestry needle. Do not cut ends off too short. In multicolour work remember to darn the end through parts of the same shade only.

Blocking a Garment
Before the garment is sewn together or the edges worked, pin out each piece to the correct measurements. Do not pin out the lower 10 cm (4 in) of a jumper or sleeves if an eding is to be worked around (Fig. 93). Check instructions for pressing the yarn on the ball band first, in any case only press lightly to avoid flattening the beautiful texture.

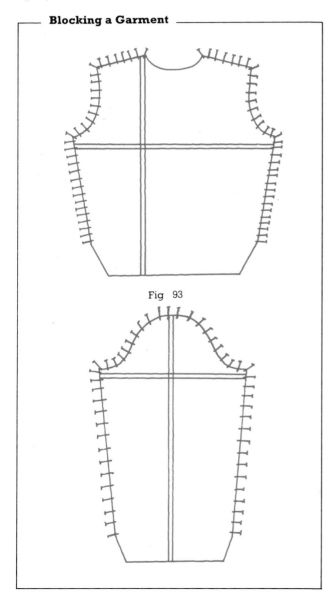

Blocking a Garment

Fig 93

Sewing-up Finished Items
After blocking and before any edgings are worked the garment is sewn together with matching yarn. Do not split the yarn as it will lose strength. Never crochet garment seams together.

Always join shoulder seams and set in sleeves with a back stitch as follows: place the 2 pieces of fabric evenly together with right sides facing inwards. Pin into position, then sew together with a row of stitches worked below the 2 top loops of each stitch of last row (Fig. 94).

Side seams and sleeve seams are joined with a flat seam. Work an over-sew stitch at the commencing chain end, then thread the needle up through the fabric to the top of the next row and work another over-sew stitch. Continue up the seam (Fig. 95). It should be possible to match the pieces perfectly this way so that the seam becomes invisible. When joining lacy patterns, notice how the stitches are matched across before the thread is pulled tight as in the case of this shell stitch (Fig. 96).

Multicolour work will need to have particular rows sewn up in their matching colour if the seam stitches are not to show.

When setting in a sleeve, divide the crown in half and mark half way point with coloured thread. Sew into position from the shoulder seam down, fasten off. Sew the other side from the shoulder seam down to match. Do the same to a collar, divide in half and sew into position from the centre back to one front corner and from the centre back to the other corner. Remember that collars fold over and the neck seam may show inside the garment so sew it especially neatly.

To make loose covers for cushions, join only 3 sides, attach 'velcro' or tape with press studs to the 4th side as a means of getting the cover on and off the cushion.

Joining Motifs
There are three ways of joining motifs: sewing them, crocheting them or actually joining them together whilst being worked. The instructions will tell you which method to use.

Sewing Motifs Together
After every motif has been completed, with the right sides of the two motifs to be joined facing inwards, join using an oversew stitch. Stitches must not be pulled tight, otherwise the work can pucker or the strain on the joining thread prove far too great once the article is in use so that it breaks. Sew all the crossways seams first and then the lengthways seams (Fig. 97).

Joining Motifs by Crochet
To crochet the motifs together after completion the same principles apply as for sewing. The right sides of both motifs being joined face inwards and a double crochet worked passing the hook through the two top loops of the first stitch on each motif, thus picking up 4 loops altogether. Continue to work a double crochet through both motifs into every stitch along edge (Fig. 98). Join all motifs across first into long strips and then lengthways (Fig. 97). The advantages of this method are that because the yarn is in a continuous length joins only occur round the edges of the article; and that a double crochet join will tend to stretch and spring back with wear.

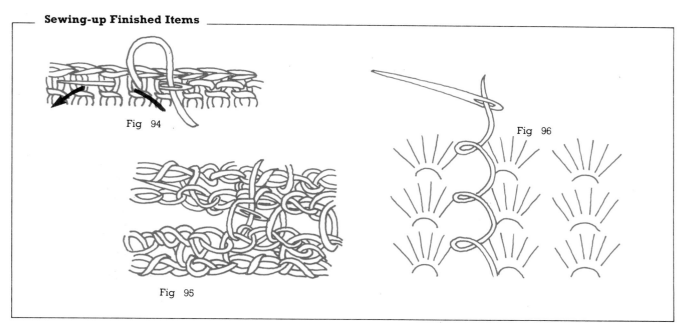

Fig 94

Fig 95

Fig 96

Joining Motifs during Working

Joining motifs whilst the final round is worked will always be described fully in the instructions. It is helpful, when a joining stitch is to be made, to place the motif being worked and the one to be joined to it, on a flat surface with right sides facing upwards. Insert the hook from the back to the front and draw a loop through (Fig. 99). In this way motifs will never twist.

Edgings

A ribbing stitch does not exist in crochet so it is the edging, which is worked after the article is made and sewn together that gives shape and a neat finish. Work edgings with right side facing unless instructions say 'turn'. On the first edging round, to avoid loops pulling and holes appearing, always try to pick up

more than one thread. For example, when working along 'other side of a commencing chain', pick up the last remaining loop of each chain and also a thread from each stitch made on the foundation row.

All edgings used have been described in full throughout this book.

Collars

Take care when sewing on collars that both sides are symmetrical and that the edging around it is not worked too tight, otherwise the collar may curl.

Buttonholes

Place buttonholes no further apart than 8 cm (3 in) and no nearer than 1 cm ($\frac{1}{2}$ in) from the edge, then the opening will not gape.

Joining Motifs

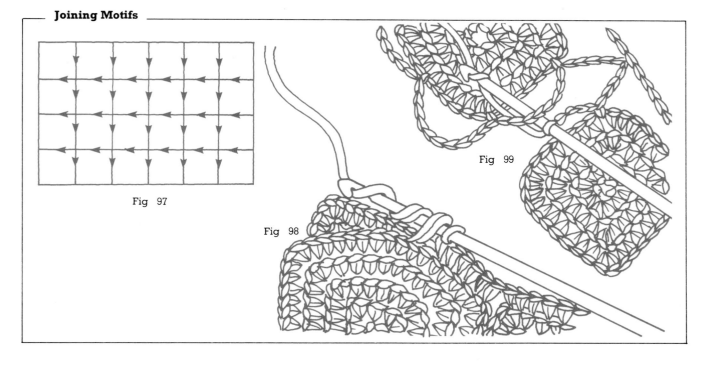

Fig 97

Fig 98

Fig 99

How to Sew in a Zip

First of all fit the garment, then pin up the opening where the zip is to be inserted and measure the opening. Do not buy a zipper longer than this measurement.

Lie the garment flat and pin the zip into position on the wrong side of work, with the ends tucked inside. Sew a row of running stitches close to the teeth, then oversew all the other edges with small stitches (Fig. 100).

How to Make a Herringbone Casing

This is the best method for sewing a band of elastic round the waist of a garment. Make the elastic into a ring, place into position and then with a darning needle and matching yarn sew herringbone stitch over the elastic (Fig. 101) taking care not to catch it, because it must be free to stretch inside the casing.

How to Make Tassels

Take a piece of cardboard as wide as the required length of tassel and wind yarn round it thickly. Press both sides using a hot iron and a damp cloth. Cut through one edge of yarn (Fig. 102). Insert hook into work where tassel is to be made, fold thread into two and draw through. Now draw the two threads through loop (Fig. 103). Tassels can be made using many threads but only one thread has been used here for clarity.

Knotting

Patterns can be made by knotting tassels together after they have been fixed into position. This takes up some of the length of the threads, so allow an extra 2·5 cm (1 in) for every row of knots. To make a knot take two threads, one from each of two different tassels, wrap threads round finger to form a ring, draw the two ends through and pull tight. Place all subsequent knots evenly along the row to match (Fig. 104).

How to Make Pompons

Take a piece of cardboard 5 cm (2 in) wide. Place two pieces of thread across the top. Wind yarn round cardboard and the two threads, until it is quite thick (Fig. 105). Tie very firmly at the top with the two threads, then cut through other edge (Fig. 106). Trim pompon into a neat circular shape and sew into position with the tied ends (Fig. 107).

How to Make Bobbles

Bobbles are good for putting on the ends of ties for baby clothes, because, unlike a tassel no threads can become loose when chewed. Use two strands of yarn. Our diagrams show only single thickness being worked so that the method of working may be clearly seen.

Yarn round finger once to form a ring, 3 ch, 10 tr into commencing ring, 1 ss into 3 rd of 3 ch (Fig. 108). Fasten off leaving a long thread hanging. Thread this through the top of each treble with a needle (Fig. 109). Draw tight and fasten off. Draw commencing ring tight and use this thread to attach bobble to cord (Fig. 110).

How to Cover Button Moulds

It is easy to spoil a garment by choosing badly matching buttons, whereas buttons covered in the same yarn as the garment really add a professional touch to any article and are never out of place.

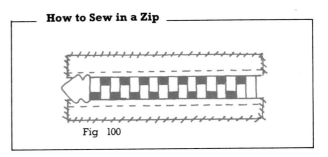

How to Sew in a Zip

Fig 100

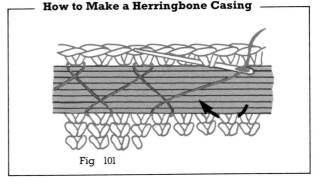

How to Make a Herringbone Casing

Fig 101

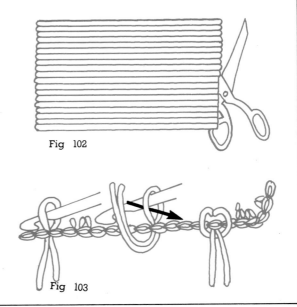

How to Make Tassels

Fig 102

Fig 103

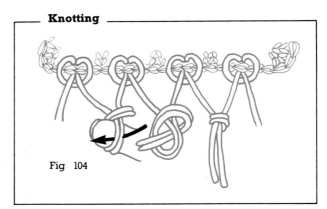

Knotting

Fig 104

How to Make Pompons

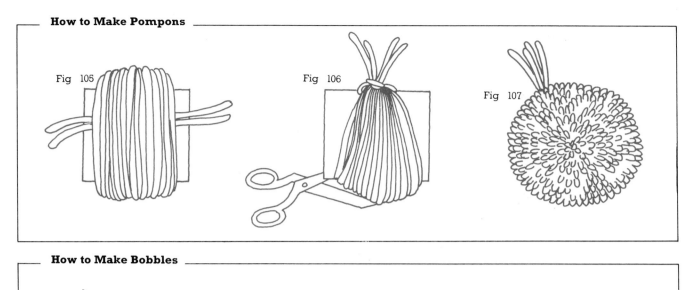

Fig 105   Fig 106   Fig 107

How to Make Bobbles

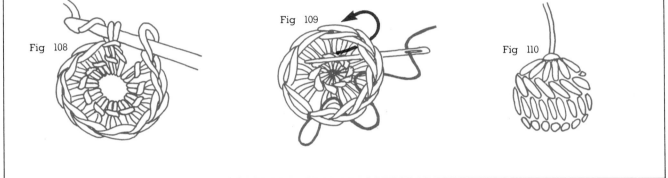

Fig 108   Fig 109   Fig 110

Using single thickness wrap yarn round finger once to form a ring, 7 dc into commencing ring, * 2 dc into next dc, 1 dc into next dc; rep from * around until circle is large enough to cover the top of the mould, end with 1 ss into next dc. Fasten off. (Fig. 111). Draw commencing ring tight. Darn in ends. Cover the mould with the crochet (Fig. 112) and then snap on the back.

Making up and Lining a Bag with Frame
Once the back and front have been made, join the lower seam. Join the side seams leaving 5 cm (2 in) unsewn at the top. The next step is to attach the crochet to the bag frame. Open the frame and beginning with the front, mark the centre of the frame and the centre of the last row of crochet. Place the crochet under the frame and sew into position working from the centre outwards and gathering up the crochet as you go along. Sew down the side of the frame. Sew the other side to match, beginning at the centre. Sew back of frame on in the same manner. Do not let the sewing stitches show on the outside of the bag frame. If it is impossible to hide the stitches, place the crochet on top of the bag frame and attach in the same way.

Cut the lining slightly larger than the bag, to allow for seams. Sew side and lower seams with a French seam so that all raw edges are enclosed. Leave the top part of each side seam unsewn, to allow for the opening. Tuck the top edge of the lining up into the bag frame with needle until the inside looks neat and sew into position.

How to Cover Button Moulds

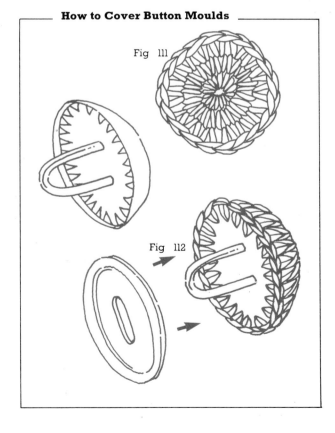

Fig 111

Fig 112

CARING FOR CROCHET

Washing

Most yarns today come with washing instructions on the ball bands. Follow these instructions but remember that crochet tends to stretch more easily than knitting because the stitches worked are longer, therefore the stitches can stretch as well as the yarn. Always be a little more careful than with knitted garments; if uncertain wash by hand.

Use lukewarm water of about 40° Centigrade and liquid soap or detergent. If a powder is used make sure that it has completely dissolved before immersing the crochet. Wash carefully, squeezing gently. Never boil (except white cotton). Do not rub a particular spot too hard otherwise the yarn will become fluffy. Do not lift crochet up out of the water because it could stretch owing to the additional weight when saturated. Rinse gently and thoroughly in cold water. Do not wring. Place a large towel on the table then carefully spread the crochet into shape on it, if any parts overhang the towel fold them in. Roll the towel and its contents up. Either leave for about 30 minutes by which time the towel will have absorbed most of the water, or pop the rolled up bundle into a spin dryer for a very short spin. Beware of spinning anything containing man-made fibres especially acrylics as they have a tendency to crease. Unroll the towel, remove the crochet to a dry towel, ease gently into shape and leave flat until dry.

Pressing

Crochet only ever needs a light press otherwise the stitches will look rather flattened. Instructions for pressing the various yarns are usually given on the ball bands, follow these carefully, especially if the yarn contains man-made fibres: some, e.g. acrylics must never be pressed. Never press the edgings of a crocheted garment, particularly jumper and cardigan edgings, because some of the natural elasticity in the yarn will be lost and the garment will tend to lose its shape easily. Always place a cloth between the article and the iron when pressing, this will prevent shiny marks being made.

Starching and Pinning Out

Cotton doilies and other fine household items look their best if pinned out and starched. This can be a rather long task but the finished result is superb.

After washing, lay the crochet on a piece of graph paper (make sure the ink lines on the paper will not run when wet) or better still use a piece of gingham fabric with a pattern of squares. Without straining the crochet, pin out the shape starting at the centre and working outwards with rustless pins, using the lines on the gingham or graph paper as guidelines to get the pattern evenly spaced. Pull out all the picots, shells and loops evenly as it is most important that crochet should look symmetrical. Dab over with liquid starch and leave to dry. Remove the pins and press lightly.

Left Pram Blanket (p. 41) and white Matinee Jacket from the pair on p. 54.

Right Matinee Jacket, Bonnet and Pram Cover (p. 44).

Inset Left Matinee Jacket (p. 40) and **Right** blue Matinee Jacket from the pair on p. 54.

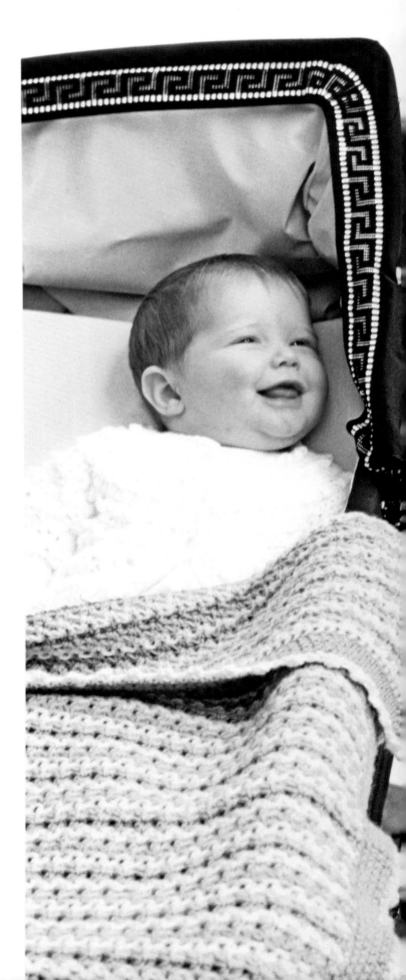

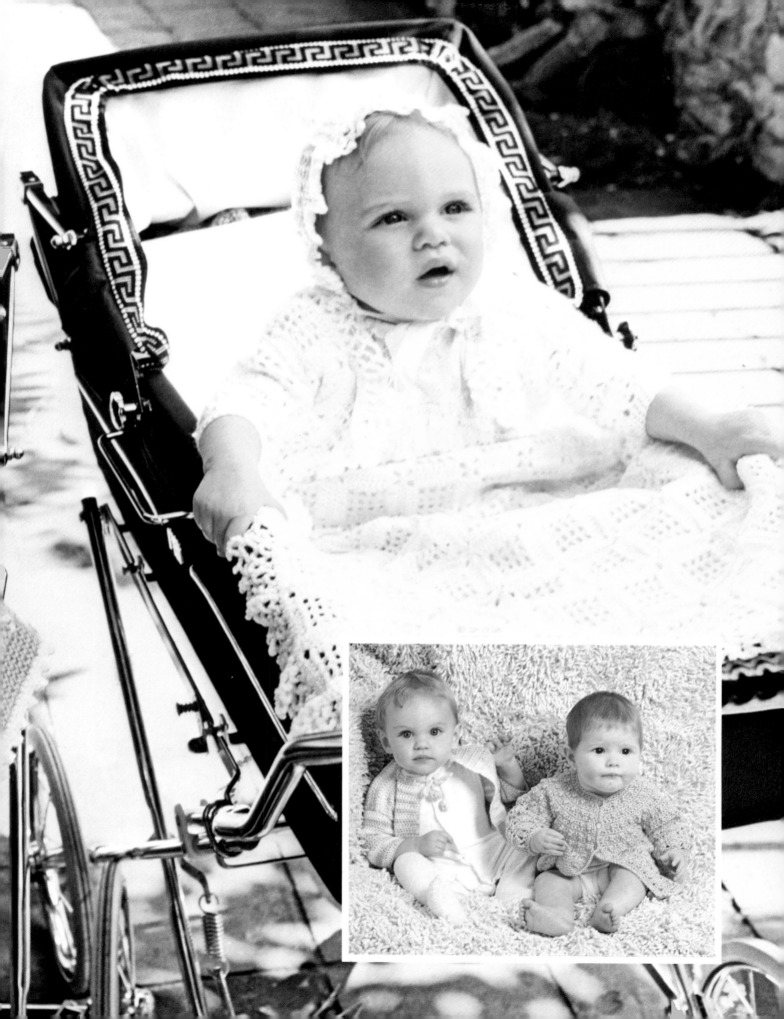

WHAT'S GONE WRONG

Crochet can sometimes turn out unsuccessfully and an inexperienced worker cannot always see why the faults have occurred or how to correct them. Listed here are the most common problems that arise.

Fault	Causes	Refer to
Squat unattractive stitches	1 Fluffy or bobbly finished yarn used 2 Yarn has an exceptional amount of elasticity 3 Yarn wound around fingers too tightly 4 Damp hands stopping the yarn from flowing smoothly	The Yarn on page 24 The Yarn on page 24 Tension on page 25 Tension on page 25
Split yarn	1 Loosely twisted yarn used 2 Crochet hook too small for the thickness of yarn 3 The hook part of the crochet hook is too sharp	The Yarn on page 24 The Hook on page 24 The Hook on page 24
Hairs, threads and soiled marks in work	1 Yarn or work not being kept clean	Keeping Work Clean on page 24
Ridges across tops of stitches	Stitches have been worked into only one of the top loops on previous row	Working the Next Rows on page 26
Article has stretched or shrunk	1 Bad washing 2 Wrong yarn used for the particular design	Washing on page 34 Materials on page 24
Article too large or small	1 Tension incorrect 2 Wrong size made 3 Wrong yarn or hook used, or both	Tension on page 25 Which Size on page 24 Materials on page 24
Garment too long	1 Inaccurate length measurements made 2 Stretched tape measure used 3 Work not held up when measuring length	Measuring Length on page 24 Measuring Length on page 24 Measuring Length on page 24
Dropped front edges of cardigan	1 Edging worked too loosely 2 Too many stitches worked on edging 3 Edging has been pressed 4 Edging stretched while wet	Edgings on page 31 Edgings on page 31 Pressing on page 34 Washing on page 34
Front of cardigan gapes	1 Width of garment too small 2 Buttonholes worked too near edge 3 Buttonholes placed too far apart	Which Size? on page 24 Buttonholes on page 31 Buttonholes on page 31
Holes appear in commencing chain when foundation row is worked	1 Uneven commencing chain 2 Foundation row has been worked into only one loop of commencing chain 3 A grouped stitch has been worked into commencing chain e.g. a shell 4 Edging not worked properly	The Commencing Chain on page 26 The Foundation Row on page 26 Edgings on page 31 Edgings on page 31
Centre of motifs loosening	1 Poor finish to the work 2 Commencing loop incorrectly made	How to Begin on page 26 How to Begin on page 26
Side edges of work slope (not motifs)	1 Increasing and decreasing stitches when not required 2 Varying tension	The Turning Chain on page 26 and Counting Stitches on page 27 Tension on page 25

Fault	Causes	Refer to
Side edges cockle	1 The last stitch of some rows is being worked into the wrong turning chain	The Turning Chain on page 26
	2 An incorrect number of turning chains have been worked	The Turning Chain on page 26
Edges of circular motifs are cockled	1 Motif is not the quoted finished size	Tension (Length) on page 25
	2 The increasings have been worked incorrectly	Tension (Length) on page 25
Corners of square motifs are not right-angles	1 Motif is not the quoted finished size	Tension (Length) on page 25
	2 Corner increasings have been worked incorrectly	Tension (Length) on page 25
Beginning of work cockled	1 Commencing chain has been worked too tight or loose	The Commencing Chain on page 26
	2 The stitch pattern tension is too loose or tight	Tension on page 25
Parts of article are inside out	1 Insufficient care at the making up stage	The Right Side of Work on page 29
	2 Motifs not joined correctly	Joining Motifs on page 30
Puckered zip	1 Sewn in incorrectly	How to Sew in a Zip on page 32
	2 The zip is too large or small for the opening	How to Sew in a Zip on page 32
Unsightly seams	1 Sewing up with the wrong stitch or yarn	Sewing-up Finished Items on page 30
	2 Rows of patterns not matched	Sewing-up Finished Items on page 30
	3 Garment seams crocheted together	Sewing-up Finished Items on page 30
	4 Motifs joined incorrectly	Joining Motifs on page 30
Garments tight at underarm	Decreasing slip stitches worked too tightly so that yarn will not give (this can cause discomfort when the garment is worn)	Decreasing and Increasing on page 28
Collar curls	1 Edging worked too tightly	Collars on page 31
	2 Collar is not symmetrical	Collars on page 31

LIST OF DESIGNS IN ORDER OF DIFFICULTY

Start by making articles at the beginning of this list and gradually advance. The tension sample, at the beginning of each design, has been described in detail in order to encourage you to check your tension. Even if you do not wish to make a particular garment it would be good practice in making the various stitches, if you worked up all of these squares. Most of the tension samples are 10 cm (4 in) square so they need not be wasted: sew them together to make an attractive blanket or cushion.

Matinee Jacket
Pull-on and Scarf
Bed Jacket
Pram Blanket
Mohair Stole
Triangular Shawl
Rectangular Cushion
Tabard
Tammy
Car Rug and Cushion
Rug
Hat with Brim
Bedspread and Matching Cushion
Shawl of Shells
Patchwork Cushion

Jacket and Baby Bag
Blouson and Skirt
Overtops
Christening Set: shawl,
long gown, short gown,
  bonnet, and bootees
Child's Jumper
Collar and Cuffs
Evening Bag
Two Matinee Jackets
Mother and Daughter Ponchos
Ponchos
Peaked Cap
Zip-up Jacket
Boy's Sets

Round Cushion and Bolster
Matinee Jacket, Bonnet and Pram Cover
Motif Table Cloth
Motif Waistcoats
Semi-circular Shawl
Layette: shawl, angel top, bonnet,
  pants, bonnet and mitts
Two Dresses for Toddlers
Waistcoat and Shoulder Bag
Long Cardigan
Jumper, Waistcoat and Skirt
Circular Cloth, Doilies and Lampshade
Motif Shawl
Victorian Blouse
Smock

Above The pattern for this charming layette can be found on p. 48. The pattern suggests back opening for the Angel Top but this can also be worn with front opening as a jacket to suit the preference of the mother or child.

Left Detail of Bonnet from the layette

Far Right The beauty of a traditional, handmade Christening Set is appreciated more than ever nowdays in an age of mass production. The pattern can be found on p. 51.

Right The short Christening Gown with matching Bootees.

MATINEE JACKET

Patons Fairytale 4 ply (20 g balls)

	cm	in
To Fit Chest	46[48·5,5,50]	18[19,20]
Length	22[24, 26]	8¾[9½,10¼]
Sleeve Seam	12[13, 14]	4¾[5,5½]
Amount Required	3[4 4]	3[4, 4]

Aero crochet hook size 4·00 mm (No 8)

Tension
20 tr to 10 cm (4 in).
To make a tension sample
commence with 22 ch, work as
Back for 13 rows. Fasten off.
 If your sample is not 10 cm
(4 in) across then refer to
Tension on page 25.

For sizes and abbreviations see
pages 24 and 25.

Back

Commence with 47[50,52] ch to
measure 24[25·5,27] cm (9½[10,
10½] in).

Foundation Row
1 tr into 4th ch from hook,
1 tr into each ch to end, turn:
45[48,50] – sts.

Patt Row
3 ch, miss first tr, 1 tr into
each tr, 1 tr into 3rd of 3 ch,
turn.
 Rep patt row until Back
measures 22[24,26] cm (8¾[9½,
10¼] in) from beginning. Fasten
off.

Fronts (both alike)

Commence with 25[27,29] ch to
measure 13[14,15] cm (5[5½,6] in).
Rep Back Foundation Row once:
23[25,27] – sts.
 Rep patt row until same No. of
rows are completed as for Back.
Fasten off.

Sleeves (both alike)

Commence with 35[37,39] ch to
measure 18[19,20] cm (7[7½,8] in).
Rep Back Foundation Row once:
32[35,37] – sts.
 Rep patt row until Sleeve
measures 12[13,14] cm (4¾[5,5½]
in) from beginning. Fasten off.
 Join side seams leaving top
9[9·5,10] cm (3½[3¾,4] in) unsewn
for armholes.
 Join shoulder seams 6·5[7,7·5] cm
(2½[2¾,3] in).
 Set in sleeves. Join sleeve seams.

Neck Edging

With right side facing attach
yarn to neck corner of right
front, 3 ch, (1 hlf tr into
neck edge, 1 ch) 18[19,20]
times, end with 1 hlf tr into
neck corner of left front.
Fasten off.

Tie

With 2 strands of yarn make a
length of ch 50 cm (20 in)
long and thread this through
neck edging to tie under chin.
Make 2 bobbles (see page 32)
and attach 1 to each end of tie.

PRAM BLANKET

Emu Scotch Superwash D.K. (25 g balls)

Amount Required
Main Colour	7
1st Contrast	5
2nd Contrast	6

	cm	in
Length	90	36
Width	61	24

Aero crochet hook size 6·00 mm (No 4)

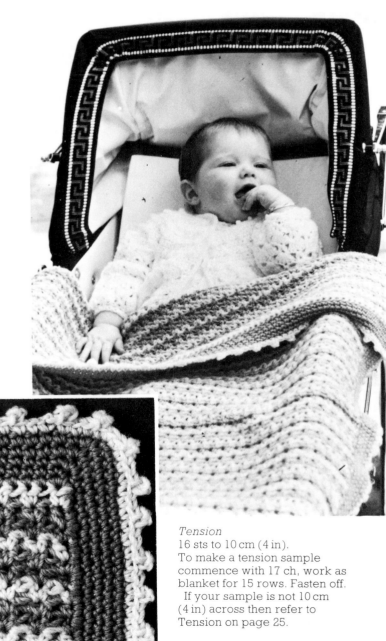

Tension
16 sts to 10 cm (4 in).
To make a tension sample
commence with 17 ch, work as
blanket for 15 rows. Fasten off.
  If your sample is not 10 cm
(4 in) across then refer to
Tension on page 25.

For abbreviations see page 25.

With C 1 commence with 89 ch to
measure 56·5 cm (22¼ in).
Foundation Row
1 hlf tr into 3rd ch from hook,
* miss next ch, 2 hlf tr into
next ch; rep from * to end,
turn: 44 – V sts.
1st Row
Attach C 2 to first sp between
2 hlf tr, 2 ch, 1 hlf tr into
same place as join, * miss next
sp, 2 hlf tr into next sp;
rep from * to end, turn.
2nd Row
Attach M to first sp between
2 hlf tr, 2 ch, 1 hlf tr into
same place as join, * miss next
sp, 2 hlf tr into next sp;
rep from * to end, turn.
3rd Row
Attach C 1 to first sp between
2 hlf tr, 2 ch, 1 hlf tr into
same place as join, * miss next
sp, 2 hlf tr into next sp;
rep from * to end, turn.
  Rep 1st to 3rd rows until
blanket is 86 cm (34 in) from
beginning, ending with 1st row.
Fasten off all colours.

Edging

1st Round
Attach M to top left corner,
3 dc into same place as join,
1 dc into each hlf tr of
last row worked, 3 dc into 2nd
corner, * 1 dc into each of next
2 row-ends, 2 dc into next
row-end; rep from * down side,
1 dc into each of last 2
row-ends, 3 dc into 3rd corner,
1 dc into each ch along lower
edge, 3 dc into 4th corner,
** 1 dc into each of next
2 row-ends, 2 dc into next
row-end; rep from ** 1 dc
into each of next 2 row-ends.
2nd to 5th Rounds
Working in continuous rounds make
* 1 dc into each dc until 2nd
dc of corner 3 dc is reached,
3 dc into next dc; rep from
* ending last round with 1 dc
into each dc, 1 ss into first
dc. Fasten off.
Last Round
Attach C 2 to same place as ss,
* 1 dc into each of next 3 dc,
3 ch, 1 ss into last dc made;
rep from * ending with 1 ss
into first dc. Fasten off.

Left Keep the children warm for a family walk with the Child's Zip-up Jacket (pattern on p. 61) and the Jacket and Baby Bag (pattern on p. 55).

Above These pretty Dresses for Toddlers (pattern on p. 59) present a complete contrast in mood. Colours should be chosen to suit the individual child, as above. A dark dress with a light contrast might be preferred for a winter dress.

MATINEE JACKET, BONNET AND PRAM COVER

Sirdar Snuggly 3 ply (20 g balls)

Amount Required	Coat and Bonnet	Cover
Main Colour	5	4
Contrast	–	3

	cm	in		cm	in
To Fit Chest	48	19	Length	66	26
Length	25	10	Width	56	22
Sleeve Seam	13	5			
Bonnet Face Edge	30·5	12			

Aero crochet hook size 3·50 mm (No 9)
Ribbon 90 cm (36 in)

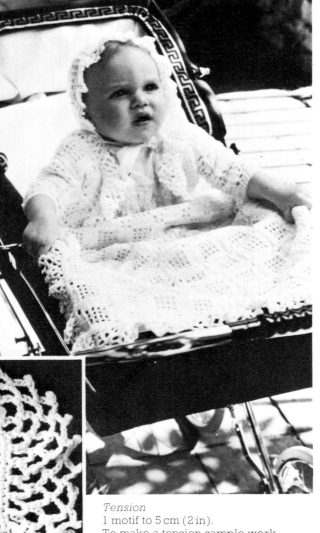

Tension
1 motif to 5 cm (2 in).
To make a tension sample work
1 motif.
  If your sample is not 5 cm
(2 in) across then refer to
Tension on page 25.

For abbreviations see page 25.

Pram Cover

Motif

With C commence with 12 ch to
measure 5 cm (2 in).

Foundation Row
1 tr into 6th ch from hook,
(1 ch, miss next ch, 1 tr into
next ch) 3 times, turn: 4 – sp.

1st Row
4 ch, miss first tr, (1 tr
into next tr, 1 ch) 3 times,
1 tr into 3rd of 4 ch, turn.
  Rep last row twice more.
Fasten off.

Edging Round
Attach M to top left corner,
7 ch, 1 tr into same place as
join, * 1 tr into corner sp,
1 tr into next st, (1 tr
into next sp, 1 tr into next
st) twice, 1 tr into corner sp,
(1 tr, 4 ch, 1 tr) into
corner; rep from * twice more,
end with 1 tr into corner sp,
1 tr into next st, (1 tr into
next sp, 1 tr into next st)
twice, 1 tr into corner sp,
1 ss into 3rd of 7 ch. Fasten
off.

Make 99 motifs altogether.

Joining Motifs

Place first 2 motifs together
with right sides facing.
Working through both motifs
attach C to corner 4 ch lp,
1 dc into same place as join,
* 2 ch, 1 dc into each of next
9 tr, 2 ch, 1 dc into next
corner 4 ch lp, take next 2
motifs with right sides facing
inwards, 1 dc into first corner
4 ch lp; rep from * 9 times
more, 2 ch, 1 dc into each of
next 9 tr, 2 ch, 1 dc into
last corner 4 ch lp. Fasten off.
Join 7 more rows of motif. Join
sides of motifs in the same
manner. 9 rows of 11 motifs.

Edging

1st Round
With right side facing attach M
to tr before any corner
4 ch lp, ** 7 dc into corner
4 ch lp, * 1 dc into each of
next 9 tr, 2 dc into each of
next 2 joined sp; rep from
* to within 9 tr before next
corner, 1 dc into each of next
9 tr **. Rep from ** to **
3 times more, ending with 1 dc
into first dc.

2nd Round
* 5 ch, miss next dc, 1 dc into next dc; rep from * to within last dc, 2 ch, 1 tr into first of 5 ch.
3rd Round
* 5 ch, 1 dc into next 5 ch lp; rep from * ending with 2 ch, 1 tr into first of 5 ch.
4th Round
1 dc into first lp, * 5 ch, 1 dc into next 5 ch lp; rep from * omitting 1 dc at end of last rep, 1 ss into first dc. Fasten off.
Last Round
Attach C to any lp, 1 dc into same place as join, * 5 ch, 1 ss into 3rd ch from hook (a picot formed), 3 ch, 1 dc into next 5 ch lp; rep from * working 1 dc at end of last rep into first dc. Fasten off.

Matinee Jacket

Using M throughout, make 50 motifs. Join as described for pram cover to the shape shown in diagram.

Join side and sleeve seams.

Edging

As pram cover edging, using M throughout and commencing at top corner of Right Front.

Cuffs (both alike)

1st Round
With right side facing attach M to sleeve, then work 27 dc evenly around edge, 1 dc into first dc.
2nd to 4th Rounds
Working in continuous rounds make 1 dc into each dc, end last round with 1 ss into next dc. Fasten off.

Slot 46 cm (18 in) length of ribbon through 3rd round of neck edging to tie under chin

Bonnet

Using M throughout, make 15 motifs. Join as described for Pram Cover to the shape shown in diagram.

Edging

1st Round
As 1st round of Pram Cover edging. Fasten off.

Face Edging

1st Row
With wrong side facing attach M to 4th of 7 dc at corner, 1 dc into same place as join, (5 ch, miss next dc, 1 dc into next dc) 39 times along face edge, 2 ch, miss next dc, 1 tr into next dc, turn.
2nd Row
1 dc into first lp, * 5 ch, 1 dc into next 5 ch lp; rep from * to within last loop, end with 2 ch, 1 tr into last lp, turn.
  Rep last row once more.
4th Row
1 dc into first lp, * 5 ch, 1 ss into 3rd ch from hook, (a picot formed), 3 ch, 1 dc into next 5 ch lp; rep from * to end. Fasten off.

Turn bonnet edging back and sew into position along neck edge. Attach 23 cm (9 in) length of ribbon to each corner to tie under chin.

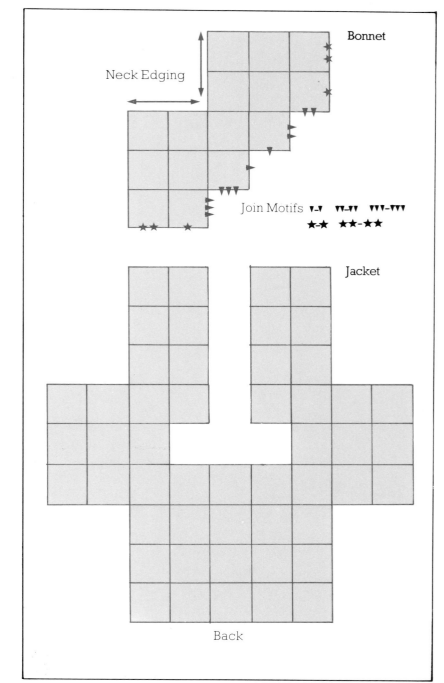

Below The Tabards (pattern on p. 72) are really comfortable and easy to wear. The mother's has been made up in a fluffy, random yarn for a lovely warm texture, whereas the daughter's is in a plain yarn to show up the attractive stitch pattern.

Right These Motif Waistcoats (pattern on p. 65) are ideal for cooler summer days. Subtle tones of pink and mauve have been used here; clever choice of the three colours can produce a really versatile addition to your wardrobe.

LAYETTE

Robin Bambino 4 ply (20 g balls)

	cm	in	Amount Required	Main Colour	Contrast
To Fit Chest	48	19	Angel Top		4
Length	30	11¾	Pants		2
Sleeve Seam	14	5½	Bootees		1
Length of Foot	9	3½	Mittens		1
Bonnet Face Edge	30·5	12	Bonnet		1
Shawl	70 × 70	42 × 42	Shawl	19	2

2 Buttons
45 cm (17½ in) of elastic
Aero crochet hook size 3·50 mm (No 9)

Tension
4 patt to 10 cm (4 in).
To make a tension sample commence with 27 ch, work as shawl centre for 9 rows. Fasten off.
 If your sample is not 10 cm (4 in) across then refer to Tension on page 25.

For abbreviations see page 25.

Shawl

Centre
With M commence with 213 ch to measure 90 cm (35½ in).

Foundation Row
4 tr into 6th ch from hook,
* miss 2 ch, 1 tr into next ch, miss 2 ch, 4 tr into next ch; rep from * ending with miss 2 ch, 1 tr into last ch, turn: 35 – shells.

1st Row
5 ch, miss first tr, * leaving last lp on hook make 1 tr into each of next 4 tr, yarn over hook and draw through all lps on hook (a cluster made), 2 ch, 1 tr into next single tr, 2 ch; rep from * omitting 1 tr and 2 ch at end of last rep, 1 tr into 3rd of 3 ch, turn.

2nd Row
3 ch, * 4 tr into next cluster, 1 tr into next single tr; rep from * to end working last 1 tr into 3rd of 5 ch, turn.
 Rep 1st and 2nd rows until centre is 89 cm (35 in) from beginning, ending with 1st row, turn.

Border

1st Round
* (2 dc into each of next two 2 ch sp, 1 dc into next single tr) 34 times, 2 dc into each of last two 2 ch sp, 4 dc into the corner st, now work 174 dc evenly along side edge, 4 dc into next corner st; rep from * once more, end with 1 ss into first dc.
 Mark centre dc at each of the 4 corners. There should be 177 dc between each marked dc.

2nd Round
3 ch, * 1 tr into each dc to centre dc at next corner, 5 tr into next dc; rep from * 3 times more, 1 ss into 3rd of 3 ch. Fasten off.

3rd Round
Attach C to same place as ss, 3 ch, * 1 tr into each tr to centre tr at next corner, 5 tr into next tr; rep from * 3 times more, 1 ss into 3rd of 3 ch. Fasten off.

4th Round
Attach M to same place as ss, then work as 3rd round. Do not fasten off.

5th Round
3 ch, (miss 2 tr, 4 tr into next tr, miss next tr, 1 tr into next tr) 36 times, * miss

2 tr, (4 tr, 1 ch, 4 tr) into corner tr, miss next tr, 1 tr into next tr, (miss 2 tr, 4 tr into next tr, miss next tr, 1 tr into next tr) 37 times; rep from * twice more, end with miss 2 tr, (4 tr, 1 ch, 4 tr) into last corner tr, miss next tr, 1 tr into next tr, miss 2 tr, 4 tr into next tr, miss next tr, 1 ss into 3rd of 3 ch.

6th Round
5 ch, (a cluster over next 4 tr, 2 ch, 1 tr into next single tr, 2 ch) 36 times, * a cluster over next 4 tr, 4 ch, 1 dbl tr into corner 1 ch sp, 4 ch, a cluster over next 4 tr, 2 ch, 1 tr into next single tr, 2 ch, (a cluster over next 4 tr, 2 ch, 1 tr into next single tr, 2 ch) 37 times; rep from * twice more, end with a cluster over next 4 tr, 4 ch, 1 dbl tr into last corner 1 ch sp, 4 ch, a cluster over next 4 tr, 2 ch, 1 tr into last single tr, 2 ch, a cluster over last 4 tr, 2 ch, 1 ss into 3rd of 5 ch.

7th Round
(2 dc into each of next two 2 ch sp, 1 dc into next single tr) 36 times, * 2 dc into next 2 ch sp, 5 dc into next 4 ch sp, 1 dc into next dbl tr, 5 dc into next 4 ch sp, 2 dc into next 2 ch sp, 1 dc into next single tr, (2 dc into each of next two 2 ch sp, 1 dc into next single tr) 37 times; rep from * twice more, end with 2 dc into next 2 ch sp, 5 dc into next 4 ch sp, 1 dc into next dbl tr, 5 dc into next 4 ch sp, 2 dc into next 2 ch sp, 1 ss into first dc.
Rep 2nd, 3rd and 4th rounds once.

Last Round
* 1 dc into each of next 3 tr, 3 ch, 1 ss into last dc made; rep from * ending with 1 ss into first dc. Fasten off.

Angel Top

Yoke

With C working from neck down commence with 45 ch to measure 24 cm (9½ in).

Foundation Row
2 tr into 4th ch from hook, * 1 tr into each of next 4 ch, 2 tr into next ch; rep from * to within last ch, 1 tr into last ch, turn: 52 – sts.

1st Row
3 ch, miss first tr, 1 tr into next tr, * 2 tr into next tr, 1 tr into each of next 5 tr; rep from * ending with 2 tr into next tr, 1 tr into 3rd of 3 ch, turn: 61 – sts.

2nd Row
3 ch, miss first tr, 1 tr into each of next 2 tr, * miss next tr, 4 tr into next tr, miss next tr, 1 tr into next tr; rep from * 13 times more, 1 tr into next tr, 1 tr into 3rd of 3 ch, turn.

3rd Row
3 ch, miss first tr, 1 tr into each of next 2 tr, * 2 ch, a cluster over next 4 tr, 2 ch, 1 tr into next single tr; rep from * 13 times more, 1 tr into next tr, 1 tr into 3rd of 3 ch, turn.

4th Row
3 ch, miss first tr, 1 tr into each of next 2 tr, * 2 tr into next 2 ch sp, 1 tr into next cluster, 2 tr into next 2 ch sp, 1 tr into next single tr; rep from * 13 times more, 1 tr into next tr, 1 tr into 3rd of 3 ch, turn.

5th Row
3 ch, miss first tr, 1 tr into each of next 2 tr, (2 tr into next tr, 1 tr into each of next 8 tr) 9 times, 2 tr into next tr, 1 tr into each of next 3 tr, 1 tr into 3rd of 3 ch, turn: 99 – sts.

Right Back

1st Row
3 ch, miss first tr, 1 tr into each of next 10 tr, (2 tr into next tr, 1 tr into each of next 2 tr) twice, 1 tr into next tr, turn: 20 – sts.

**2nd Row
3 ch, miss first tr, * 1 tr into each tr until next 2 tr group is reached, 2 tr into next tr; rep from * ending with 1 tr into each tr, 1 tr into 3rd of 3 ch, turn.
Rep last row 7 times more.

Patt Row
3 ch, miss first tr, 1 tr into each tr, 1 tr into 3rd of 3 ch, turn.
Rep last row until work is 23 cm (9 in) from beginning.

1st Insert Row
3 ch, miss first tr, * miss 2 tr, 4 tr into next tr, miss next tr, 1 tr into next tr; rep from * working 1 tr at

end of last rep into 3rd of 3 ch, turn.

2nd Insert Row
As 1st row of Shawl Centre.

3rd Insert Row
3 ch, miss first tr, * 2 tr into next 2 ch sp, 1 tr into next cluster, 2 tr into next 2 ch sp, 1 tr into next tr; rep from * working 1 tr at end of last rep into 3rd of 3 ch, turn
Rep patt row until work is 30 cm (11½ in) from beginning. Fasten off. **.

Front

Miss next 14 sts for armhole and attach C to next tr, 3 ch, (1 tr into each of next 2 tr, 2 tr into next tr) twice, 1 tr into each of next 21 tr, (2 tr into next tr, 1 tr into each of next 2 tr) twice, 1 tr into next tr, turn: 39 – sts.
Rep from ** to ** of Right Back once. (71 sts after all the inc rows have been worked.)

Left Back

Miss next 14 sts for 2nd armhole and attach C to next tr, 3 ch, (1 tr into each of next 2 tr, 2 tr into next tr) twice, 1 tr into each of next 10 tr, 1 tr into 3rd of 3 ch, turn: 20 – sts.
Rep from ** to ** of Right Back once.

Join side seams leaving top 4 rows unsewn for armholes.

Sleeves (both alike)

1st Round
With right side facing attach C to base of armhole, 3 ch, 3 tr into each of next 4 row-ends, 1 tr into each of next 14 tr across yoke, 3 tr into each of next 4 row-ends down other side, 1 ss into 3rd of 3 ch, turn: 39 – sts.

2nd Round
3 ch, 1 tr into each tr, 1 ss into 3rd of 3 ch, turn.
Rep last round until sleeve is 13 cm (5 in) from beginning.

Next Round
* 1 dc into next tr, miss next tr; rep from * ending with 1 dc into 3rd of 3 ch, 1 dc into first dc.

Last Round
* 3 ch, 1 ss into last dc made,

continued overleaf

49

1 dc into each of next 2 dc;
rep from * ending with 1 ss
into first dc. Fasten off.

Pants

Back

Working from waist down with C
commence with 49 ch to measure
25 cm (10 in).
Foundation Row
1 tr into 4th ch from hook,
1 tr into each ch to end, turn: 47 – sts.
 Rep Angel Top patt row until
work is 11 cm (4½ in) from
beginning.
Shape Crotch
1st Row
Miss first tr, 1 ss into next
tr, 3 ch, 1 tr into each tr
to within last 2 sts, turn:
3 – sts decreased.
 Rep last row 8 times more:
20 – sts remain. Fasten off.

Front

As Back to Shape Crotch.
Shape Crotch
1st Row
Miss first tr, 1 ss into each
of next 5 sts, 3 ch, 1 tr into
each tr to within last 5 sts,
turn: 10 – sts decreased.
2nd Row
Miss first tr, 1 ss into next
tr, 3 ch, 1 tr into each tr
to within last st, turn: 2 – sts
decreased.
 Rep last row 7 times more.
Fasten off.

Bonnet

Wrap C round finger once to form
a ring.
1st Row
3 ch, 18 tr into commencing
ring. Draw commencing ring tight,
turn.
2nd Row
3 ch, 1 tr into first tr,
2 tr into each tr, 1 tr into
3rd of 3 ch, turn: 37 – sts.
3rd Row
3 ch, miss first tr, 1 tr into
next tr, (2 tr into next tr,
1 tr into each of next 2 tr)
11 times, 2 tr into next tr,
1 tr into 3rd of 3 ch, turn:
49 – sts.
 Rep Angel Top Right Back 2nd row
once, patt row 6 times, 1st and
2nd Insert rows once: 12 – patt.
Next Row
3 ch, * 2 tr into each of next

2 sp, 1 tr into next single
tr; rep from * working 1 tr
at end of last rep into 3rd of
5 ch, turn.
 Rep patt row once. Fasten off.

Bootees (both alike)

With C commence with 16 ch to
measure 8 cm (3¼ in).
1st Round
2 tr into 3rd ch from hook,
1 tr into each of next 12 ch,
3 tr into last ch, then working
along other side of commencing
ch make 1 tr into each of next
12 ch, 1 ss into 3rd of 3 ch:
30 – sts.
2nd Round
3 ch, 1 tr into next tr, 3 tr
into next tr, 1 tr into each
of next 14 tr, 3 tr into next
tr, 1 tr into each of next
12 tr, 1 ss into 3rd of 3 ch:
34 – sts.
3rd Round
3 ch, 1 tr into each tr, 1 ss
into 3rd of 3 ch.
4th Round
3 ch, 1 tr into each of next
15 tr, leaving last lp on hook
make 1 tr into each of next
6 tr, yarn over hook and draw
through all lps on hook (a dec
formed), 1 tr into each of next
12 tr, 1 ss into 3rd of 3 ch: 29 – sts.
5th Round
3 ch, 1 tr into each tr to
within 2 tr before next dec,
a dec over next 6 sts, 1 tr
into each tr, 1 ss into 3rd of
3 ch: 24 – sts.
6th Round
4 ch, miss next tr, * 1 tr
into next tr, 1 ch, miss next
tr; rep from * ending with
1 ss into 3rd of 4 ch: 12 – sp.
7th Round
3 ch, * 1 tr into next 1 ch sp,
1 tr into next tr; rep from
* ending with 2 tr into last
1 ch sp, 1 ss into 3rd of
3 ch; 25 – sts.
8th Round
3 ch, * miss 2 tr, 4 tr into
next tr, miss next tr, 1 tr
into next tr; rep from *
omitting 1 tr at end of last
rep, 1 ss into 3rd of 3 ch.
9th Round
3 ch, * 2 ch, a cluster over
next 4 tr, 2 ch, 1 tr into
next single tr; rep from *
omitting 1 tr at end of last
rep, 1 ss into 3rd of 5 ch.
10th Round
3 ch, * 2 tr into next 2 ch sp,

1 tr into next cluster, 2 tr
into next 2 ch sp, 1 tr into
next tr; rep from * omitting
1 tr at end of last rep, 1 ss
into 3rd of 3 ch.
11th Round
* 1 dc into each of next 2 tr,
3 ch, 1 ss into last dc made;
rep from * ending with 1 dc
into first dc. Fasten off.

Mittens (both alike)

With C commence with 13 ch
tightly to measure 4 cm (1½ in).
1st Round
2 tr into 3rd ch from hook,
1 tr into each of next 9 ch,
3 tr into next ch, then working
along other side of commencing
ch make 1 tr into each of next
9 ch, 1 ss into 3rd of 3 ch.
 Rep 3rd round of Bootees 8 times
then 6th to 11th round once each.
Fasten off.

Finishing

Join Bonnet seam 8 cm (3 in).
Join pants side and crotch seams.

For the Angel Top neck edging
proceed as follows:
with right side facing attach C
to edge, * 2 dc evenly into
edge, 3 ch, 1 ss into last
dc made; rep from * round neck,
left and right back and lower
edge, end with 1 ss into first
dc. Fasten off.
 Work edging to match round waist
and legs of pants and round bonnet.

Sew elastic to waist of pants
with a herringbone casing (see
page 32).

With 2 strands of C make 4
lengths of ch 45 cm (17½ in) long
and thread these through 6th
round of bootees and mittens.
Make 2 lengths of ch 22 cm (8½ in)
long and sew one to each corner
of bonnet.
 Make and attach bobbles to all
ends (see page 32).

Sew buttons down back of Angel
Top using sp between sts as
buttonholes. □

CHRISTENING SET

Templetons H and O Shetland Lace 3 ply (25 g balls)

	cm	in	Amount Required
Shawl	70 × 70	42 × 42	11
To Fit Chest	48	19	
Long Gown Length	60	23½	6
Short Dress Length	35	14	3
Length of Foot	9	3½	1
Bonnet Face Edge	30	12	1

Aero crochet hook size 3·50 mm (No 9)
Buttons for gown and dress
Narrow baby ribbon

Tension
24 tr and 12 rows to 10 cm (4 in).
To make a tension sample
commence with 26 ch, work as
shawl centre for 12 rows. Fasten
off.
 If your sample is not 10 cm (4 in)
across then refer to tension on
page 25.

For abbreviations see page 25

Shawl

Centre
Commence with 212 ch to measure
90 cm (35½ in).
Foundation Row
1 tr into 4th ch from hook,
1 tr into each ch to end, turn:
210 − sts.
1st Row
3 ch, miss first tr, 1 tr into
each tr, 1 tr into 3rd of 3 ch, turn.
 Rep last row 103 times more, turn.

Border

1st Round
1 dc into first tr, 1 dc into
each of next 208 tr, 1 dc into
3rd of 3 ch, 2 dc into each
row-end, 1 dc into each of next
210 ch, 2 dc into each row-end,
1 ss into first dc.
2nd Round
4 ch, * (miss next dc, 1 tr
into next dc, 1 ch) 105 times,
miss next dc, (1 tr, 1 ch)
3 times into next dc; rep from
* twice more, end with (miss next
dc, 1 tr into next dc, 1 ch)
105 times, miss next dc, (1 tr,
1 ch) twice into same place as
ss, 1 ss into 3rd of 3 ch.
Fasten off.
 Mark tr at centre of each
corner: 107 − 1 ch sp on each
edge.
3rd Round
Attach yarn to any marked corner
tr, 3 ch, (2 tr, 1 ch, 4 tr)
into same place as join, * (2 tr
into each of next two 1 ch sp,
1 ch, miss next 1 ch sp,
2 tr into each of next two
1 ch sp, 4 tr into next
1 ch sp) 17 times, 2 tr into
each of next two 1 ch sp, 1 ch,
miss next 1 ch sp, 2 tr into
each of next two 1 ch sp,
(4 tr, 1 ch, 4 tr) into
marked tr; rep from * twice
more, end with (2 tr into each
of next two 1 ch sp, 1 ch,
miss next 1 ch sp, 2 tr
into each of next two
1 ch sp, 4 tr into next
1 ch sp) 17 times, 2 tr into
each of next two 1 ch sp, 1 ch,
miss next 1 ch sp, 2 tr into
each of next two 1 ch sp,
1 tr into same place as join,
1 ss into 3rd of 3 ch.
4th Round
Working into sp between sts
make (1 ss, 3 ch, 2 tr) into

continued overleaf

next sp, * 1 tr into next sp,
1 ch, miss next 1 ch sp, 1 tr
into next sp, (4 tr into next
sp, 1 tr into each of next
4 sp, 1 ch, miss next 3 sp,
1 tr into each of next 4 sp)
18 times, 4 tr into next sp;
rep from * 3 times more,
omitting 4 tr at end of last
rep, 1 tr into same place
as ss made at beginning of row,
1 ss into 3rd of 3 ch.

5th Round
(1 ss, 3 ch, 2 tr) into next
sp, * 1 tr into each of next
2 sp, 1 ch, miss next 1 ch sp,
1 tr into each of next 2 sp,
(4 tr into next sp, 1 tr into
each of next 4 sp, 1 ch, miss
next 3 sp, 1 tr into each of
next 4 sp) 18 times, 4 tr into
next sp; rep from * 3 times
more omitting 4 tr at end of
last rep, 1 tr into same place
as ss, 1 ss into 3rd of 3 ch.

6th Round
(1 ss, 3 ch, 2 tr) into next
sp, * 1 tr into each of next
3 sp, 1 ch, miss next 1 ch sp,
1 tr into each of next 3 sp,
(4 tr into next sp, 1 tr into
each of next 4 sp, 1 ch, miss
next 3 sp, 1 tr into each of
next 4 sp) 18 times, 4 tr into
next sp; rep from * 3 times
more omitting 4 tr at end of
last rep, 1 tr into same place
as ss, 1 ss into 3rd of 3 ch.

7th Round
(1 ss, 3 ch, 2 tr) into next
sp, * 1 tr into each of next
4 sp, 1 ch, miss next 1 ch sp,
1 tr into each of next 4 sp,
(4 tr into next sp, 1 tr into
each of next 4 sp, 1 ch, miss
next 3 sp, 1 tr into each of
next 4 sp) 18 times, 4 tr into
next sp; rep from * 3 times
more omitting 4 tr at end of
last rep, 1 tr into same place
as ss, 1 ss into 3rd of 3 ch.

8th Round
(1 ss, 3 ch, 2 tr) into next
sp, * 1 tr into each of next
4 sp, 1 ch, miss next sp,
4 tr into next 1 ch sp, 1 ch,
miss next sp, 1 tr into each
of next 4 sp, (4 tr into next
sp, 1 tr into each of next
4 sp, 1 ch, miss next 3 sp,
1 tr into each of next 4 sp)
18 times, 4 tr into next sp;
rep from * 3 times more omitting
4 tr at end of last rep, 1 tr
into same place as ss, 1 ss
into 3rd of 3 ch.

9th Round
(1 ss, 3 ch, 2 tr) into next

sp, * 1 tr into each of next
4 sp, 1 ch, miss 2 sp, 1 tr
into next sp, 4 tr into next
sp, 1 tr into next sp, 1 ch,
miss 2 sp, 1 tr into
each of next 4 sp, (4 tr
into next sp, 1 tr into each
of next 4 sp, 1 ch, miss next
3 sp, 1 tr into each of next
4 sp) 18 times, 4 tr into next
sp; rep from * 3 times more
omitting 4 tr at end of last
rep, 1 tr into same place as
ss, 1 ss into 3rd of 3 ch.

10th Round
(1 ss, 3 ch, 2 tr) into next
sp, * 1 tr into each of next
4 sp, 1 ch, miss 2 sp, 1 tr
into each of next 2 sp, 4 tr
into next sp, 1 tr into each
of next 2 sp, 1 ch, miss 2 sp,
1 tr into each of next 4 sp,
(4 tr into next sp, 1 tr into
each of next 4 sp, 1 ch, miss
next 3 sp, 1 tr into each of
next 4 sp) 18 times, 4 tr into
next sp; rep from * 3 times
more omitting 4 tr at end of
last rep, 1 tr into same place
as ss, 1 ss into 3rd of 3 ch.

11th Round
(1 ss, 3 ch, 2 tr) into next
sp, * 1 tr into each of next
4 sp, 1 ch, miss 2 sp, 1 tr
into each of next 3 sp, 4 tr
into next sp, 1 tr into each
of next 3 sp, 1 ch, miss 2 sp,
1 tr into each of next 4 sp,
(4 tr into next sp, 1 tr into
each of next 4 sp, 1 ch, miss
next 3 sp, 1 tr into each of
next 4 sp) 18 times, 4 tr into
next sp; rep from * 3 times
more omitting 4 tr at end of
last rep, 1 tr into same place
as ss, 1 ss into 3rd of 3 ch.

12th Round
(1 ss, 3 ch, 2 tr) into next
sp, * (1 tr into each of next
4 sp, 1 ch, miss 2 sp, 1 tr
into each of next 4 sp, 4 tr
into next sp) twice, (1 tr into
each of next 4 sp, 1 ch, miss
next 3 sp, 1 tr into each of
next 4 sp, 4 tr into next sp)
18 times; rep from * 3 times
more omitting 4 tr at end of
last rep, 1 tr into same place
as ss, 1 ss into 3rd of 3 ch.

Last Round
Ss to last tr before next
1 ch sp, * 1 dc into next
1 ch sp, (1 dc into each of
next 2 sp, 3 ch, 1 ss into
last dc made) 3 times, 1 dc
into same place as last dc,
1 dc into next sp, (3 ch,
1 ss into last dc made, 1 dc

into each of next 2 sp) twice;
rep from * ending with 1 ss
into first dc. Fasten off.

Long Gown And Short Dress

Yoke

Commence with 71 ch tightly
to measure 23 cm (9 in).
Foundation Row
1 tr into 4th ch from hook,
1 tr into each of next 15 ch,
3 tr into next ch, 1 tr into
next ch, 3 tr into next ch,
1 tr into each of next 29 ch,
3 tr into next ch, 1 tr into
next ch, 3 tr into next ch,
1 tr into each of last 17 ch,
turn: 77 – sts.

1st Row
3 ch, miss first tr, * 1 tr
into each tr to within centre
tr of next 3 tr group, 3 tr
into next tr; rep from * 3
times more, 1 tr into each tr,
1 tr into 3rd of 3 ch, turn.
  Rep last row 4 times more:
117 – sts.

Right Back

1st Row
3 ch, miss first tr, (1 ch,
miss next tr, 1 tr into next
tr) 10 times, turn.
** 2nd Row For Long Gown Only
3 ch, 1 tr into first tr,
* 2 tr into each of next two
1 ch sp, 4 tr into next tr;
rep from * ending with 2 tr
into each of next two 1 ch sp,
2 tr into 3rd of 4 ch, turn.

**2nd Row For Short Dress Only
3 ch, 1 tr into first tr,
* 2 tr into next 1 ch sp, 1 ch,
2 tr into next 1 ch sp, 4 tr
into next 1 ch sp, 2 tr into
next 1 ch sp, 1 ch, 2 tr into
next 1 ch sp, 4 tr into next
tr; rep from * omitting 4 tr
at end of last rep, end with
2 tr into 3rd of 4 ch.

3rd Row for Both Versions
3 ch, 1 tr into first tr,
* 1 tr into each of next 3 sp,
1 ch, miss next sp, 1 tr
into each of next 3 sp, 4 tr
into next sp; rep from *
omitting 4 tr at end of last
rep 2 tr into 3rd of 3 ch,
turn.

4th Row
3 ch, 1 tr into first tr, *
1 tr into each of next 4 sp,
1 ch, miss next 1 ch sp, 1 tr
into each of next 4 sp, 4 tr
into next sp; rep from *

omitting 4 tr at end of last
rep, 2 tr into 3rd of 3 ch,
turn.

5th Row

3 ch, 1 tr into first tr,
* 1 tr into each of next 4 sp,
1 ch, miss 3 sp, 1 tr into
each of next 4 sp, 4 tr into
next sp; rep from * omitting
4 tr at end of last rep, 2 tr
into 3rd of 3 ch, turn.

   Rep 5th row until work measures
60 cm (23½ in) from beginning
for Long Gown and 35 cm (14 in)
for Short Gown. Fasten off. **.

Front

1st Row

Miss next 17 ch for armhole,
attach yarn to next tr, 3 ch,
(miss next tr, 1 ch, 1 tr into
next tr) 20 times, turn.

   Rep from ** to ** of Right Back
once.

Left Back

1st Row

Miss next 17 ch for 2nd armhole,
attach yarn to next tr, 3 ch,
(miss next tr, 1 ch, 1 tr into
next tr) 9 times, miss next
tr, 1 ch, 1 tr into 3rd of
3 ch, turn.

   Rep from ** to ** of Right Back
once.

Join side and back seams leaving
top 5 rows of skirt open for
armholes and back opening.

Sleeves (both alike)

1st Round

With right side facing attach
yarn to base of armhole, 3 ch,
then make 14 tr along armhole
edge, 1 tr into each of next
17 tr across yoke, 14 tr down
other side, 1 ss into first tr.

2nd Round

3 ch, 1 tr into each tr, 1 ss
into 3rd of 3 ch.

3rd Round

1 dc into first tr, (miss next
tr, 1 dc into each of next
3 tr) 11 times, 1 dc into last st.

Last Row

(1 dc into each of next 2 dc,
3 ch, 1 ss into last dc made)
17 times, miss last dc, 1 ss into
first dc. Fasten off.

Lower Edge of Dresses

Rep last round of Shawl once.
Fasten off.

Neck and Back Opening Edging

With right side facing attach
yarn to base of back opening, up
back work * 2 dc into next
row-end, 3 ch, 1 ss into last
dc made; rep from * to corner,
2 dc into corner, ** 3 ch,
1 ss into last dc made, miss
next st, 1 dc into each of
next 2 sts; rep from ** to 2nd corner,
complete to match first side.
Fasten off. Sew 3 buttons down back.

Bonnet

Commence with 4 ch, 1 ss into
first ch to form a ring.

1st Row

3 ch, 10 tr into commencing
ring: 11 – sts.

2nd Row

3 ch, miss first tr, 3 tr into
each tr, 3 tr into 3rd of 3 ch,
turn: 31 – sts.

3rd Row

4 ch, miss first 2 tr, (1 tr
into next tr, 1 ch, miss next
tr) 13 times, 1 tr into 3rd of
3 ch, turn: 15 – sp.

   Rep from ** to ** of Short Dress
until bonnet is 15 cm (6 in)
from beginning. Fasten off.

Bonnet Edging

Join bonnet seam 8 cm (3 in).
With right side facing attach
yarn to back seam, along side
edge work * 2 dc into next
row-end, 3 ch, 1 ss into last
dc made; rep from * to corner,
across face edge work 1 dc into
first tr, ** 1 dc into next sp,
(3 ch, 1 ss into last dc made,
1 dc into each of next 2 sp)
twice, 1 dc into each of next
3 sp, (3 ch, 1 ss into last
dc made, 1 dc into each of
next 2 sp) twice, 3 ch, 1 ss into
last dc made, 1 dc into same place
as last dc; rep from ** to 2nd
corner, complete to match first
side, 1 ss into first dc. Fasten off.

Bootees (both alike)

Commence with 19 ch to measure
8 cm (3¼ in).

1st Round

2 tr into 3rd ch from hook,
1 tr into each of next 15 ch,
3 tr into last ch, then working
along other side of commencing
ch make 1 tr into each of next
15 ch, 1 ss into 3rd of 3 ch.

2nd Round

3 ch, 1 tr into next tr, 3 tr

into next tr, 1 tr into each of
next 17 tr, 3 tr into next tr,
1 tr into each of next 15 ch,
1 ss into 3rd of 3 ch: 40 – sts.

   Rep 2nd round of Dress Sleeves
twice.

5th Round

3 ch, 1 tr into each of next
18 tr, leaving last lp on hook
make 1 tr into each of next
6 tr, yarn over hook and draw
through all lps on hook (a dec
made), 1 tr into each of next
15 tr, 1 ss into 3rd of 3 ch.

6th Round

3 ch, 1 tr into each tr to
within 2 tr before dec, a dec
over next 6 sts, 1 tr into each
tr, 1 ss into 3rd of 3 ch.

7th Round

4 ch, miss next tr, * 1 tr
into next tr, 1 ch, miss next
tr; rep from * ending with
1 ss into 3rd of 4 ch: 15 –
1 ch sp.

8th Round

3 ch, 2 tr into same place as
ss, * 2 tr into each of next
2 sp, 1 ch, miss next sp,
2 tr into each of next 2 sp,
4 tr into next tr; rep from
* twice more omitting 4 tr at
end of last rep, 1 tr into same
place as ss, 1 ss into 3rd of
3 ch.

9th Round

1 ss into next sp, 3 ch, 2 tr
into same place as ss, * 1 tr
into each of next 4 sp, 1 ch,
miss next 3 sp, 1 tr into each
of next 4 sp, 4 tr into next
tr; rep from * twice more
omitting 4 tr at end of last
rep, 1 tr into same place as
ss, 1 ss into 3rd of 3 ch.

   Rep last round once more, then
rep last round of Shawl once.
Fasten off.

Finishing

Slot ribbon through back and
front of dress and gown yoke
and sew into position.

   Thread 46 cm (18 in) of ribbon
through each bootee to tie at
front.

   Sew a 30 cm (12 in) length of
ribbon to each corner of bonnet
to tie under chin.   □

TWO MATINEE JACKETS

Sirdar Snuggly Quick Knit (20 g balls)

Amount Required		6
	cm	in
To Fit Chest	51	20
Length	28	11
Sleeve Seam	14	5½

Aero crochet hooks sizes 4·00 mm and 4·50 mm (No 8 and No 7 respectively)
3 buttons

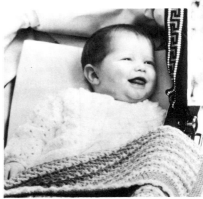

Tension
2 patt to 7·5 cm (3 in). To make a tension sample commence with 15 ch, work as back for 8 rows. Fasten off.

If your sample is not 7·5 cm (3 in) across then refer to Tension on page 25.

For abbreviations see page 25.

Turquoise Jacket

Back

With 4·50 mm (No 7) hook commence with 51 ch to measure 33 cm (13 in).

Foundation Row

5 tr into 6th ch from hook (a shell formed), * miss 2 ch, 2 tr into next ch, miss 2 ch, 5 tr into next ch (another shell formed); rep from * ending with miss 2 ch, 1 tr into last ch, turn: 8 – shells.

Patt Row

3 ch, miss first 3 tr, * 5 tr into next tr, miss 3 tr, 2 tr into next sp, miss 3 tr; rep from * ending with 5 tr into next tr, 1 tr into 3rd of 3 ch, turn.

Rep patt row until back is 15 cm (6 in) from beginning. Fasten off.

Fronts (both alike)

With 4·50 mm (No 7) hook commence with 27 ch to measure 18 cm (7 in). Work to match back: 4 – shells.

Sleeves (both alike)

With 4·50 mm (No 7) hook commence with 33 ch to measure 22 cm (8½ in). Work as for Back until sleeve is 13 cm (5 in). Fasten off: 5 – shells.

**Yoke

1st Row

With 4·00 mm (No 8) hook attach yarn to first tr at corner of right front, 1 dc into same place as join, (1 dc into each of next 2 tr, miss next tr, 1 dc into each of next 3 tr, miss next tr) 3 times, 1 dc into each of next 5 tr, 1 dc into 3rd of 3 ch (22 – dc), 1 dc into first tr of sleeve, (1 dc into each of next 2 tr, miss next tr, 1 dc into each of next 4 tr) 4 times, 1 dc into each of next 5 tr, 1 dc into 3rd of 3 ch (31 – dc), 1 dc into first tr of back, (1 dc into each of next 2 tr, miss next tr, 1 dc into each of next 3 tr, miss next tr) 7 times, 1 dc into each of next 2 tr, miss next tr, 1 dc into each of next 2 tr, 1 dc into 3rd of 3 ch (41 – dc), now work across 2nd sleeve and front to match 1st sleeve and right front, turn: 147 – dc altogether.

2nd Row

* 1 dc into next dc, 1 dbl tr into next dc, 1 dc into next dc; rep from * to end, turn.

3rd Row

* 1 dc into next dc, 1 dc into next dbl tr, 1 dc into next dc; rep from * to end, turn.

4th Row

(1 dc into each of next 3 dc, miss next dc, 1 dc into each of next 3 dc) 21 times, turn: 126 – dc.

5th Row

1 dc into each dc to end, turn.
Rep 2nd and 3rd rows once.

8th Row

(1 dc into each of next 3 dc, miss next dc, 1 dc into each of next 2 dc) 21 times, turn: 105 – dc.
Rep 5th, 2nd and 3rd rows once.

12th Row

(1 dc into each of next 2 dc, miss next dc, 1 dc into each of next 2 dc) 21 times, turn: 84 – dc.
Rep 5th, 2nd and 3rd rows once.

16th Row

(1 dc into each of next 2 dc, miss next dc, 1 dc into next dc) 21 times, turn: 63 – dc.
Rep 5th, 2nd and 3rd rows once.

Last Row

(1 dc into next dc, miss next dc, 1 dc into next dc) 21 times. Fasten off: 42 – dc.

Join side and sleeve seams.

Edging

1st Round

With 4·00 mm (No 8) hook and right

side facing attach yarn to any seam on lower edge, 1 dc into each ch, 3 dc into corner, 2 dc into each tr row-end, 1 dc into first dc row-end, (2 ch, miss next 2 dc row-ends, 1 dc into each of next 6 dc row-ends) twice, 2 ch, miss next 2 dc row-ends, 3 dc into corner, * 1 dc into each of next 2 dc, miss next dc; rep from * round neck edge, 3 dc into corner, 1 dc into each dc row-end, 2 dc into each tr row-end, 3 dc into corner, 1 dc into each ch, 1 dc into first dc.

2nd Round
1 dc into each st, 1 ss into first dc. Fasten off.

Cuffs (both alike)

1st Round
With 4·50 mm (No. 7) hook and right side facing attach yarn to any ch, 1 dc into same place as join, * miss next ch, 1 dc into next ch; rep from * ending with 1 dc into first dc.
 Rep 2nd Round of Edging once.
 Sew buttons down yoke to correspond with buttonholes. **.

White Jacket

Back

As Turquoise Jacket Back until Foundation Row is completed.
1st Row
3 ch, 2 tr into first tr, miss 2 tr, * 2 tr into next tr, miss 3 tr, 5 tr into next sp, miss 3 tr; rep from * ending with 2 tr into next tr, 3 tr into 3rd of 3 ch, turn.
2nd Row
3 ch, miss first tr, * miss 3 tr, 5 tr into next sp, miss 3 tr, 2 tr into next tr; rep from * ending with miss 3 tr, 5 tr into next tr, 1 tr into 3rd of 3 ch, turn.
 Rep last 2 rows until back is 15 cm (6 in) from beginning ending with 2nd row. Fasten off.

Fronts (both alike)

With 4·50 mm (No 7) hook commence with 27 ch to measure 18 cm (7 in). Work to match back: 4 – shells.

Sleeves (both alike)

With 4·50 mm (No. 7) hook commence with 33 ch to measure 22 cm (8½ in). Work as for Back until sleeve is 13 cm (5 in). Fasten off. 5 – shells.
 Now work from ** to ** of Turquoise Jacket once.

JACKET AND BABY BAG

Emu Mix and Match double double (50 g balls)

	cm	in	
To Fit Chest	48 [51, 53]	19 [20 , 21]	
Jacket Length	26 [28, 30]	10 [11, 12]	
Bag Length	60 [60, 60]	23½ [23½, 23½]	
Sleeve Seam	13 [15, 17]	5 [6 , 7]	

Jacket	Amount Required		
Main Colour	4 [4, 5]	4 [4, 5]	An open-
Contrast	1 [1, 1]	1 [1 , 1]	ended zip
Baby Bag			
Main Colour	7 [7, 8]	7 [7 , 8]	An ordinary
Contrast	2 [2, 2]	2 [2 , 2]	zip

Aero crochet hook size 8·00 mm (No 1)

Tension
11 sts to 10 cm (4 in).
To make a tension sample commence with 12 ch, work as Back for 8 rows. Fasten off.
 If your sample is not 10 cm (4 in) across then refer to Tension on page 25.

For sizes and abbreviations see pages 24 and 25.

continued overleaf

55

Jacket

Back

Working from side seam with M commence with 30[32,34] ch to measure 26[28,30] cm (10¼[11, 11¾] in).

Foundation Row
1 dc into 2nd ch from hook, * 1 tr into next ch, 1 dc into next ch; rep from * to end, turn.

1st Patt Row
1 dc into front lp of first dc, * 1 tr round front of next tr, 1 dc into front lp of next dc; rep from * to end, turn.

2nd Patt Row
1 dc into back lp of first dc, * 1 tr round back of next tr, 1 dc into back lp of next dc; rep from * to end, turn.
   Rep 1st and 2nd patt rows until Back is 28[29,30] cm (11[11½, 12] in) from beginning. Fasten off.

Left and Right Fronts (both alike)

As Back until Foundation Row is completed. Fasten off and turn.

**1st Row
Attach C to front lp of first dc, 1 dc into same place as join, * 1 tr round front of next tr, 1 dc into front lp of next dc; rep from * to end. Fasten off and turn.

2nd Row
Attach M to back lp of first dc, 1 dc into same place as join, * 1 tr round back of next tr, 1 dc into back lp of next dc; rep from * to end. Fasten off and turn.
   Rep last 2 rows once more. Do not fasten off at end of last row. **.
   Rep 2nd and 1st patt rows until Front is 14[14·5,15] cm (5½[5¾, 6] in) from beginning. Fasten off.

Join shoulder seams leaving first 6[6,7] rows of each front unsewn for neck.

Sleeves (both alike)

Mark 7th[8th,8th] dc either side of shoulder seams.

1st Row
With right side facing attach M to marked dc, 1 dc into same place as join, (1 tr round back of next tr, 1 dc into next dc) 5[6,6] times, 1 tr round back of next tr, 1 dc into shoulder seam, (1 tr round back of next tr, 1 dc into next dc) 6[7,7] times, turn.
   Rep 1st and 2nd patt rows until sleeve is 7[9,11] cm (2½[3½, 4½] in) from beginning ending with 2nd patt row. Fasten off and turn.
   Rep from ** to ** of Front once.

Next Row
Attach C to first dc, 1 dc into same place as join, * miss next st, 1 dc into next st; rep from * to end, turn.

Last Row
1 dc into each dc to end. Fasten off.

Hood

Working from face edge with M commence with 42[46,50] ch to measure 38[41,44] cm (15[16¼, 17½] in).
   As Back until Foundation Row is completed. Fasten off and turn. Rep from ** to ** of Front once. Rep 1st and 2nd patt rows until work is 13[14,15] cm (5[5½,6] in). Fasten off.

Back Gusset

1st Row
With right side facing miss first 7[8,9] dc and attach M to back lp of next dc, 1 dc into same place as join, (1 tr round back of next tr, 1 dc into back lp of next dc) 6 times, turn.
   Rep 1st and 2nd patt rows until gusset is 13[14,15] cm (5[5½, 6] in) from beginning. Fasten off.

Join hood seams. Join side and sleeve seams. Sew hood to neck edge matching the stripes on hoods and fronts.

Edging

1st Round
With right side facing attach C to lower edge, then work 1 dc into each row-end, 3 dc into corner, * 1 dc into each of next 3 ch, miss next ch; rep from * up front, round face edge and down 2nd front, 3 dc into next corner, 1 dc into each row-end, 1 dc into first dc.

2nd Round
1 dc into each dc all round, 1 ss into first dc. Fasten off. ***.
   Sew an open-ended zip down front opening (see page 32).

Baby Bag

Work as for Jacket to *** but for Back and Fronts commence with 64 ch for all sizes to measure 60 cm (23½ in).

Lower Panel

Work as for Jacket Back until work is 8 cm (3¼ in). Fasten off.

Sew panel to lower edge. Sew an ordinary zip to front opening.   □

BOY'S SET

Sirdar Wash 'n' Wear 4 ply (20 g balls)

	cm	in
To Fit Chest	48[51, 54]	19[20, 2]
Jumper Length	21[23, 25]	8¼[9, 9¾]
Sleeve Seam	13[15, 17]	5[6, 7]
Pants Depth	11[12·5, 14]	4½[5, 5½]
Bibbed Pants Length	28[32, 36]	11[12½, 14]
Socks Foot Length	8[10, 12]	3¼[4, 4¾]

Amount Required for the Set		
Main Colour	4[4, 5]	4[4, 5]
1st Contrast	2[2, 2]	2[2, 2]
2nd Contrast	2[2, 2]	2[2, 2]

One extra ball in Main Colour is needed for the set with bib.

5 buttons for jumper
2 buttons for pants with bib
50 cm (19½ in) of elastic for pants
Aero crochet hook size 3·50 mm (No 9)

Tension
20 tr to 10 cm (4 in).
To make a tension sample commence with 22 ch, work as Pants for 11 rows. Fasten off.
 If your sample is not 10 cm (4 in) across then refer to Tension on page 25.

For sizes and abbreviations see pages 24 and 25.

Pants (both versions)

Back (both versions)
Working from waist down with M commence with 50[53,56] ch to measure 26[27,28] cm (10[10½, 11] in).
Foundation Row
1 tr into 4th ch from hook, 1 tr into each ch to end, turn: 48[51,54] – sts.
Patt Row
3 ch, miss first tr, 1 tr into each tr, 1 tr into 3rd of 3 ch, turn.
 Rep last row until Back is 10[10,13] cm (4[4,5] in) from beginning (adjust length here).

Shape Crotch
Dec Row
Miss first tr, 1 ss into next tr, 3 ch, 1 tr into each tr to within last 2 sts, turn: 3 – sts dec.
 Rep last row 11 times more. Fasten off.

Pants with Bib Only
1st Row
Working along other side of commencing ch, miss first 7 sts and attach M to next st, 3 ch, 1 tr into each ch to within last 7 sts, turn.
 Rep dec row 5[6,6] times.
 Rep patt row 6[6,7] times.

Strap

1st Row
1 dc into first st, 1 dc into next st, turn.
 Rep last row until strap is 9[10,11] cm (3½[4,4½] in) from beginning.
Last Row
4 ch, 1 ss into last dc.
Fasten off.
 Work 2nd strap to match at other end.

Front (both versions)

As Back to Shape Crotch

Shape Crotch
1st Row
Miss first tr, 1 ss into each of next 7 sts, 3 ch, 1 tr into each tr to within last 7 sts, turn.
 Rep dec row 6[7,7] times. Fasten off.

Pants with Bib Only
Rep 1st row of Back Bib once.
Rep dec row 5[6,6] times.
Rep patt row 4[4,5] times.
Fasten off.

Pants Leg Edging (both alike)
Join pants side and crotch seams.
1st Round
With right side facing attach M to side seam, 1 dc into each st, 2 dc into each tr row-end, 1 dc into each st, 1 dc into first dc.
2nd Round
1 dc into each dc all round,

continued overleaf

1 ss into first dc. Fasten off.

Top of Pants Without Bib

1st Round
With right side facing attach M
to edge, then work 1 dc into
each st, 1 dc into first dc.
  Rep 2nd round of Leg Edging
once.

Pants With Bib Edging

1st Round
With right side facing attach M
to centre back of bib, then work
1 dc into each tr to strap, up
strap miss first dc row-end,
1 dc into each dc row-end,
5 dc into next 4 ch lp, down
strap make 1 dc into each dc
row-end, 2 dc into each tr
row-end, across underarm make
1 dc into each tr, up 2nd side
make 2 dc into each tr row-end,
3 dc into corner, across front
make 1 dc into each tr, 3 dc
into 2nd corner, down side make
2 dc into each tr row-end,
across 2nd underarm make 1 dc
into each tr, now complete to
match first side, end with 1 dc
into first dc.

2nd Round
1 dc into each dc to within
3rd dc at end of 1st strap,
3 dc into next dc (1 dc into
each dc to within 2nd dc at
corner 3 dc into next dc) twice, 1 dc
into each dc to within 3rd dc
at end of 2nd strap, 3 dc into
next dc, 1 dc into each dc,
end with 1 ss into first dc.
Fasten off.

Sew buttons to pants and use
4 ch lp at end of straps as
buttonholes.
  Embroider initials to front of
bib in C 1 with a chain stitch.
Sew elastic to waist of pants
without bib and with a herringbone
casing (see page 32).

Jumper

Back

With M commence with 50[53,
56] ch to measure 26[27,28] cm
(10[10½,11] in).
Foundation Row
1 tr into 4th ch from hook,
1 tr into each ch to end, turn.
1st Patt Row
Attach C 1 to first tr, 1 dc
into same place as join, 1 dc into
each tr, 1 dc into 3rd of 3 ch, turn.

2nd Patt Row
Attach C 2 to first dc, 3 ch,
1 tr into each dc to end, turn.
  Rep 1st and 2nd patt rows
changing to M, C 1 and C 2 in
rotation throughout.
  When work is 13[14,15] cm (5[5½,
6] in) from beginning ending with
2nd patt row shape sleeves.
Shape Sleeves
Attach a 2nd thread to beginning
of last row and make 22[27,32]
ch. Fasten off.
1st Row
With original yarn make 23[28,
33] ch, 1 dc into 2nd ch from
hook, 1 dc into each of next
21[26,31] ch, 1 dc into each
st, 1 dc into each of next
22[27,32] ch, turn.
  Rep 2nd and 1st patt rows until
sleeves are 8[10,12] cm (3[4,
4½] in) from beginning. Fasten off.

Right Front

With M commence with 26[28,
30] ch to measure 13[14,15] cm
(5[5½,6] in).
Work as Back to Shape Sleeves.
Shape Sleeve
1st Row
Make 23[28,33] ch, 1 dc into 2nd ch
from hook, 1 dc into each of
next 21[26,31] ch, 1 dc into
each st to end, turn.
  Rep patt rows until one more row is
completed than for Back
Fasten off.

Left Front

As Right Front to Shape Sleeve
Shape Sleeve
Attach a 2nd thread to beginning
of last row and make 22[27,
32] ch. Fasten off.
1st Row
With original yarn make 1 dc
into each st, 1 dc into each
of next 22[27,32] ch, turn.
  Complete as for Right Front.

Join jumper side seams. Join
shoulder seams leaving centre
9[10,11] cm (3¾[4,4¼] in) unsewn
for neck.

Jumper Edging

1st Round
With right side facing attach C 1
to lower edge, then work * 1 dc
into each of next 3 ch, miss
next ch; rep from * to corner,
3 dc into corner, up side work
2 dc into each tr row-end,
3 dc into corner, round neck

work ** 1 dc into each of next
2 sts, miss next st; rep from
** to corner, 3 dc into corner,
complete to match 1st side, end
with 1 dc into first dc.
2nd Round
* 1 dc into each dc to 2nd dc
at corner, 3 dc into next dc;
rep from * 3 times more, end
with 1 ss into first dc. Fasten
off.

Cuffs (both alike)

1st Round
With right side facing attach C 1
to edge, then work 1 dc into
each row-end, 1 dc into first
dc.
  Rep 2nd round of Leg Edging
once.

Sew buttons down front of jumper.
and use sp between sts in patt
for buttonholes.

Socks (2 alike)

With M commence with 17[19,
19] ch to measure 8[9,9] cm
(3¼[3¾,3¾] in).
1st Round
2 tr into 3rd ch from hook,
1 tr into each of next 13[15,
15] ch, 3 tr into last ch,
then working along other side of
commencing ch make 1 tr into
each of next 13[15,15] ch, 1 ss
into 3rd of 3 ch: 32[36,36] – sts.
2nd Round
3 ch, 3 tr into next tr, 1 tr
into each of next 15[17,17] tr,
3 tr into next tr, 1 tr into
each of next 14[16,16] tr, 1 ss
into 3rd of 3 ch: 36[40,40] –
sts.

For 3rd Size Only
Rep last round once more:
44 – sts.
For All Sizes
Next Round
3 ch, 1 tr into each tr, 1 ss
into 3rd of 3 ch: 36[40,44] –
sts.

For 2nd and 3rd Sizes Only
Rep last round once more.
For All Sizes
Next Round
Mark tr at centre front. 3 ch,
1 tr into each tr to within
5 tr before marked st,
1 dbl tr into each of next 2 tr,
leaving last lp on hook make
1 dbl tr into each of next
6 tr, yarn over hook and draw
through all lps on hook (a dec
formed), 1 dbl tr into each of

next 2 tr, 1 tr into each tr,
1 ss into 3rd of 3 ch: 31[35,
39] – sts.
Next Round
3 ch, 1 tr into each tr to
within 5 sts before dec,
1 dbl tr into each of next 2 tr,
a dec over next 6 sts,
1 dbl tr into each of next
2 tr, 1 tr into each tr, 1 ss
into 3rd of 3 ch: 27[31,35] –
sts.
For 2nd and 3rd Sizes Only
Next Round
1 dc into each tr to within
3[5] sts before dec, 1 tr into
each of next 2 tr, leaving last
lp on hook make 1 dbl tr into
each of next 3[5] sts, yarn
over hook and draw through all
lps on hook, 1 tr into each of
next 2 tr, 1 dc into each dc,
1 ss into first dc: 29[31] –
sts.
All Sizes
Next Round
1 dc into each st, 1 ss into
first dc: 27[29,31] – sts.
Next Round
Attach C 1 to first st, 3 ch,
1 tr into each st, 1 ss into
3rd of 3 ch.
  Rep last 2 rounds changing to
C 2, M and C 1 in rotation at
end of every round until sock
from colour change is: –

For Short Socks
4[5,6] cm (1½[2,2½] in).
For Longer Socks
8[10,12] cm (3¼[4,4¾] in).
Fasten off.

□

TWO DRESSES FOR TODDLERS

Robin Columbine 4 ply crepe (20 g balls)

	cm	in
To Fit Chest	54[56,60]	21[22,23]
Length	36[41,46]	14[16,18]
Short Sleeve	3[4, 5]	2[2½, 3]
Long Sleeve	18[20,22]	7[8, 9]
Amount Required	6[7, 8]	6[7, 8]
1 ball in contrast for Long Sleeved version		

Aero crochet hook size 4·00 mm (No 8)
2 buttons

Tension
20 tr to 10 cm (4 in).
To make a tension sample
commence with 22 ch, work as
Back for 11 rows. Fasten off.
  If your sample is not 10 cm
(4 in) across then refer to
Tension on page 25.

For sizes and abbreviations
see pages 24 and 25.

Long Sleeved Version

Back

With M commence with 59[61,63]
ch to measure 29[30·5,32] cm
(11½[12,12½] in).
Foundation Row
1 tr into 4th ch from hook,
1 tr into each ch to end, turn:
57[59,61] – sts.
Patt Row
3 ch, miss first tr, 1 tr into
each tr, 1 tr into 3rd of 3 ch, turn.
  Rep patt row 6[8,10] times more.

continued overleaf

**Shape Armholes

1st Row
Miss first st, 1 ss into each of next 5 sts, 3 ch, 1 tr into each tr to within last 5 sts, turn.
2nd Row
Miss first st, 1 ss into each of next 2 sts, 3 ch, 1 tr into each tr to within last 2 sts, turn.
   Rep last row once more.

Back Opening 1st Side
Mark tr at centre of row.
1st Row
3 ch, miss first tr, 1 tr into each tr to within marked tr, turn.
   Rep patt row until armhole is 9[10,11] cm (3½[4,4½] in) from beginning. Fasten off.

Back Opening 2nd Side
1st Row
Attach M to first tr after marked tr, 3 ch, 1 tr into each tr, 1 tr into 3rd of 3 ch, turn.
   Complete as first side.

Skirt

1st Row
Working along other side of commencing ch attach M to first ch, 3 ch, * 1 ch, miss next ch, 1 tr into next ch; rep from * to end, turn: 28[29, 30] – sp.
2nd Row
1 dc into first st, 1 dc into each of next 5[6,7] sts, 1[2, 1] dc into next st, * 1 dc into each of next 10 sts, 1[2, 2] dc into next st; rep from * twice more, 1 dc into each of next 10 sts, 1[2,1] dc, next st, 1 dc into each of last 6[7,8] sts, turn: 57[64,64] – dc.
3rd Row
1 dc into first dc, * 1 dc into each of next 2 dc, 7 ch, miss 3[4,4] dc, 1 dc into each of next 3 dc; rep from * to end, turn: 7 – lps.
4th Row
1 dc into first dc, * 2 ch, 11 tr into next 7 ch lp, 2 ch, miss next 2 dc, 1 dc into next dc; rep from * to end, turn.
5th Row
3 ch, * 1 tr into each of next 11 tr, 1 tr into next dc; rep from * to end, turn.
6th Row
1 dc into first tr, * miss next sp, 1 dc into next sp, (1 dc into next tr, 1 dc into next sp) 4 times, 3 ch, 1 dc into next sp, (1 dc into next tr, 1 dc into next sp) 4 times,

miss next tr, 1 dc into next tr; rep from * working 1 dc at end of last rep into 3rd of 3 ch, turn.
7th Row
3 ch, miss first dc, * 2 ch, miss 2 dc, 1 dc into each of next 4 dc, 7 ch, miss next 6 dc, 1 dc into each of next 4 dc, 2 ch, miss 2 dc, 1 tr into next dc; rep from * to end, turn.
8th Row
1 dc into first tr, * 2 ch, 11 tr into next 7 ch lp, 2 ch, 1 dc into next tr; rep from * working 1 dc at end of last rep into 3rd of 5 ch, turn.
   Rep 5th to 8th rows until work is 27[32,37] cm (10½[12½,14½] in) ending with 5th row.
* With C rep 6th row once, with M rep 7th, 8th and 5th rows once; rep from * twice more, with C rep 6th row once. Fasten off. **

Front

As for Back to Back Opening. Rep patt row until 2 rows less than back are completed.
***Shape Neck
(1st Side)
1st Row
3 ch, miss first tr, 1 tr into each of next 9[10,11] tr, turn.
   Rep patt row twice. Fasten off.
2nd Side
1st Row
Attach M to 10th[11th,12th] st counting from other side, 3 ch, 1 tr into each tr, 1 tr into 3rd of 3 ch, turn.
   Rep patt row twice. Fasten off.

Skirt

As for Back Skirt. ***

Sleeves (both alike)

With M commence with 27[31,31] ch to measure 14[15,15] cm (5½[6,6] in).
   Rep Back Foundation Row once: 25[29,29] sts.
   Rep patt row once.
Inc Row
3 ch, 1 tr into first tr, 1 tr into each tr, 2 tr into 3rd of 3 ch, turn: 2 sts – increased.
   Rep last 2 rows 4[4,5] times more: 35[39,41] sts.
   Rep patt row until sleeve is 10[11,12] cm (4[4½,5] in) from beginning.

Shape Top
Rep Armhole Shaping 1st row once, 2nd row 3[4,5] times. Fasten off.

Cuff

Rep Skirt 1st row once: 12[14, 14] – sp.
2nd Row
1 dc into first tr, (1 dc into next 1 ch sp, 1 dc into next tr) 11[13,13] times, 1 dc into last sp, 1 dc into 3rd of 4 ch, turn.
3rd Row
1 dc into first dc, * 1 dc into each of next 2 dc, 7 ch, miss next 1[2,2] dc, 1 dc into each of next 3 dc; rep from * to end, turn.
   Rep 4th to 8th Skirt rows once, 5th row once, with C 6th row once. Fasten off.

Finishing

Join side and shoulder seams. Set in sleeves. Join sleeve seams.

Neck and Back Opening Edging

1st Row
With right side facing attach M to base of back opening, 1 dc into same place as join, 2 dc into each row-end up back, 3 dc into corner, 34[37,40] dc round neck, 3 dc into 2nd corner, 2 dc into each row-end to base, turn.
2nd Row
(1 dc into each dc to centre dc at next corner, 3 dc into next dc) twice, 1 dc into each dc to end, turn.
Last Row
* 1 dc into each of next 3 dc, 3 ch, 1 ss into last dc made; rep from * all round. Fasten off.

Overlap edging at base and sew into position. Sew 2 buttons down back and use sp in patt as buttonholes.

Waist Tie

With 2 strands of M make a length of ch 90 cm (36 in). Thread this through Skirt 1st row to tie at centre front. Make 2 bobbles and attach 1 to each end. (See page 00.) ****

Sleeve Ties (both alike)

With 2 strands of M make a length of ch 35 cm (13¾ in). Thread this through Cuff 1st row to tie at top. Complete to match waist tie.

Short Sleeved Version

Use M throughout.

Back

As Long Sleeved Version Back until patt row is worked once.
  Rep from ** to ** once.

Front

As Long Sleeved Version Back until Back Opening is reached.
  Rep patt row until 2 rows less than Back are completed.
  Rep from *** to *** once.

Sleeves (both alike)

Commence with 37[41,45] ch to measure 19[20,21] cm (7½[8,8½] in).
Foundation Row
As Back Foundation Row: 35[39, 43] – sts.
  Rep patt row 1[2,3] times.
Shape Top
Rep Back Armhole Shaping 1st row once, then 2nd row 3[4,5] times. Fasten off.

Rep from **** to **** of Long Sleeved Version once.

Sleeve Edgings (both alike)

With right side facing attach yarn to any ch, 1 dc into same place as join, 1 dc into next dc, * 3 ch, 1 ss into last dc made, 1 dc into each of next 2 dc, miss next dc; rep from * ending with 1 ss into first dc. Fasten off.

ZIP-UP JACKET

Patons Husky Pure Wool Chunky Knitting (50 g balls)

	cm	in
To Fit Chest	61[66,71]	24 [26, 28]
Length	39[41,43]	15½[16¼,17]
Sleeve Seam	32[35,38]	12½[13¾,15]
Amount Required	11[12,13]	11 [12, 13]

Open-ended zip
Aero crochet hooks sizes 7·00 mm and 8·00 mm (No 2 and No 0 respectively)

Tension
10 sts to 10 cm (4 in) with 7·00 mm (No. 2) hook.
To make a tension sample commence with 11 ch, work as Back for 10 rows. Fasten off.
  If your sample is not 10 cm (4 in) across then refer to Tension on page 25.

For sizes and abbreviations see pages 24 and 25.

continued overleaf

Back

With 7·00 mm (No 2) hook,
working from side seam commence
with 37[41,45] ch to measure
39[41,43] cm (15½[16¼,17] in).
Foundation Row
1 hlf tr into 3rd ch from hook,
1 hlf tr into each ch to end,
turn: 36[40,44] – sts.
Patt Row
2 ch, miss first sp, * 2 hlf tr
into next sp (a V st formed),
miss next sp; rep from * ending
with 1 hlf tr into 2nd of 2 ch,
turn: 17[19,21] – V sts.
  Rep patt row until Back is
34[37,40] cm (13½[14½,15½] in)
from beginning. Fasten off.

Pocket Linings (both alike)

With 7·00 mm (No 2) hook
commence
with 14[16,18] ch.
Foundation Row
1 dc into 2nd ch from hook,
1 dc into each ch to end, turn:
13[15,17] – dc.
1st Row
1 dc into first dc, 1 dc into
each dc to end, turn.
  Rep last row until work is
10[11,12] cm (4[4¼,4¾] in) from
beginning. Fasten off.

Right Front

With 7·00 mm (No. 2) hook and
working from centre commence
with 38[42,46] ch to measure
39[41,43] cm (15½[16¼,17] in).
Foundation Row
Change to 8·00 mm (No 0) hook,
1 dc into 2nd ch from hook,
* 1 tr into mext ch, 1 dc
into next ch; rep from * to
end, turn: 18[20,22] – tr.
1st Row
1 dc into front lp of first
dc, * 1 tr round front of next
tr, 1 dc into front lp of
next dc; rep from * to end,
turn.
2nd Row
1 dc into back lp of first
dc, * 1 tr round back of next
tr, 1 dc into back lp of next
dc; rep from * to end, turn.
  Rep last 2 rows until Front is
10[11,12] cm (4[4¼,4¾] in) ending
with a 2nd row. **
Inserting Pocket Row
With 7·00 mm (No 2) hook make
2 ch, miss first dc and tr,
2 hlf tr into both lps of next
dc, then working across pocket
lining only miss first dc,

(2 hlf tr into next dc, miss
next dc) 6[7,8] times,
continuing across main part miss
next 6[7,8] dc, 2 hlf tr into
each of next 10[11,12] dc,
1 hlf tr into last dc, turn:
17[19,21] – V sts.
  Rep patt row until Front is
17[18·5,20] cm (6¾[7¼,7¾] in)
from beginning. Fasten off.

Left Front

As Right Front to **.
Inserting Pocket Row
With 7·00 mm (No 2) hook make
2 ch, miss first dc and tr,
2 hlf tr into both lps of each
of next 10[11,12] dc, then
working across pocket lining only
miss next dc, (2 hlf tr into
next dc, miss next dc) 6[7,
8] times, continuing across main
part miss next 6[7,8] dc,
2 hlf tr into next dc,
1 hlf tr into last dc, turn.
  Complete as for Right Front.

Join shoulder seams leaving
6[6·5,7] cm (2¼[2½,2¾] in) unsewn
each side of neck.

Left Sleeve

With 7·00 mm (No 2) hook and right
side facing attach yarn to centre
sp of 8th[9th,10th] V st on
edge of Left Front counting from
shoulder seam, 2 ch, (miss next
sp, 2 hlf tr into next sp)
7[8,9] times, 2 hlf tr into
shoulder seam, across back work
7[8,9] V sts, then 1 hlf tr
to match front, turn: 15[17,
19] – V sts.
  Rep patt row until Sleeve is
28[30·5,33] cm (11[12,13] in)
ending with a right side row.
Cuff
1st Row
1 dc into first hlf tr, miss
next sp, (1 tr into next sp,
1 dc into next sp) 14[16,
18] times, 1 tr into next sp,
1 dc into 2nd of 2 ch, turn.
  Rep 1st and 2nd rows of Right
Front until Sleeve is 36[39,
42] cm (14[15¼,16½] in) from
beginning.
Next Row
Working into both lps of each
dc make 1 dc into first dc,
* 1 dc into next tr, 1 dc
into next dc; rep from * to
end, turn.
Last Row
1 dc into first dc, 1 dc into
each dc to end. Fasten off.

Right Sleeve

Work to match Left Sleeve.

Hood

With 8·00 mm (No 0) hook working
from face edge commence with
50[52,54] ch to measure 51[53·5,
56] cm (20[21,22] in).
Foundation Row
As Right Front Foundation Row:
24[25,26] – tr.
  Continue as Right Front to **.
Next Row
2 ch, miss first dc and tr,
2 hlf tr into both lps of each
of next 23[24,25] dc, 1 hlf tr
into last dc, turn.
  Rep patt row until Hood is
16·5[17,17·5] cm (6½[6¾,7] in).
Fasten off.
Gusset
1st Row
Miss first 8 V sts, attach yarn
to centre of next V st, 2 ch,
(miss next sp, 2 hlf tr into
next sp) 5[6,7] times, miss next
sp, 1 hlf tr into next sp,
turn.
  Rep patt row until gusset is
19 cm (7½ in) from beginning.
Fasten off.

Join side and sleeve seams. Join
hood seams. Join hood to neck
edge. Sew pocket linings into
position.

Edging

1st Round
With 7·00 mm (No. 2) hook and with
right side facing attach yarn to
lower edge, then work 1 dc into
each row-end, 3 dc into corner,
* 1 dc into each of next 3 ch,
miss next ch; rep from * up
front, round face edge and then
down 2nd front, 3 dc into next
corner, 1 dc into each row-end,
1 dc into first dc.
2nd Round
1 dc into each dc all round,
1 ss into first dc. Fasten off.

Sew zip to front opening
(see page 32).

CHILD'S JUMPER

Lister Lady Love DK (50 g balls)

	cm	in
To Fit Chest	61[66,71,76]	24 [26,28,30]
Length	38[43,48,53]	15 [17,19,21]
Sleeve Seam	32[36,38,41]	12½[14,15,16]
Amount Required	5[5, 6, 6]	5 [5, 6, 6]

Aero crochet hook sizes 4·00 mm and 3·50 mm (No 8 and No 9 respectively)
3 buttons

Tension
16 tr to 10 cm (4 in) with 4·00 mm (No 8) hook.
To make a tension sample commence with 18 ch, work as Back for 10 rows. Fasten off.
If your sample is not 10 cm (4 in) across then refer to Tension on page 25.

For sizes and abbreviations see pages 24 and 25.

Back

With 4·00 mm (No 8) hook commence with 57[61,65,69] ch to measure 36[38,41,43] cm (14[15,16,17] in).
Foundation Row
1 tr into 4th ch from hook, 1 tr into each ch to end, turn: 55[59,63,67] – sts.
Patt Row
3 ch, miss first tr, 1 tr into each tr, 1 tr into 3rd of 3 ch, turn.
Rep last row until Back is 24[29,34,39] cm (9½[11½,13½, 15½] in).
Shape Armholes
1st Row
Miss first st, 1 ss into each of next 4[4,5,5] sts, 3 ch, 1 tr into each tr to within last 4[4,5,5] sts, turn.
2nd Row
Miss first tr, 1 ss into next st, 3 ch, 1 tr into each tr to within turning ch, turn.
Rep last row 3 times more, then rep patt row an even[even,odd, odd] No. of times until armhole is 13[14,15,16] cm (5[5½,6,6½] in) from beginning. Fasten off.

Front

As Back to Shape Armhole.
Divide for Opening
Mark 3 tr at centre of row.
Shape Armhole
1st Row
Miss first st, 1 ss into each of next 4[4,5,5] sts, 3 ch, 1 tr into each tr to within marked tr, turn.
2nd Row
3 ch, miss first tr, 1 tr into each tr to within turning ch, turn.
3rd Row
Miss first st, 1 ss into next st, 3 ch, 1 tr into each tr, 1 tr into 3rd of 3 ch, turn.
Rep last 2 rows once more.
Continue as for Back to within last 3[3,4,4] rows.

Shape Neck
1st Row
3 ch, miss first tr, 1 tr into each tr to within last 4[5,5,6] sts, turn.
Rep 3rd and 2nd Armhole Shaping rows once.
For 3rd and 4th Sizes Only
Rep patt row once.

continued overleaf

For All Sizes
Fasten off.
2nd Side, Shape Armhole
1st Row
Miss 3 marked tr, attach yarn
to next tr, 3 ch, 1 tr into
each tr to within last 4[4,5,
5] sts, turn.
 Rep 3rd and 2nd Front Armhole
Shaping rows twice, then
continue as for first side to
Neck Shaping.
Shape Neck
Miss first st, 1 ss into each
of next 4[5,5,6] sts, 3 ch,
1 tr into each tr, 1 tr into
3rd of 3 ch, turn.
 Rep 2nd and 3rd rows of Front
Armhole Shaping once.
For 3rd and 4th Sizes Only
Rep patt row once.
For All Sizes
Fasten off.

Sleeves (both alike)

With 4·00 mm (No 8) hook
commence with
34[34,36,36] ch to measure
21[21,23,23] cm (8½[8½,9,9] in).
Foundation Row
1 tr into 4th ch from hook,
1 tr into each ch to end, turn:
32[32,34,34] – sts.
 Rep patt row twice.
**Inc Row
3 ch, 1 tr into first tr, 1 tr
into each tr, 2 tr into 3rd of
3 ch, turn: 2 – tr increased.
 Rep patt row 4 times. **.
Rep from ** to ** 2[3,3,4] times
more then rep inc row once.
Rep patt row until Sleeve is
30[34,36,39] cm (11¾[13¼,14¼,
15¼] in) from beginning.
Shape Top
Rep 1st row of Back Armhole
Shaping once, then rep 2nd row
of Back Armhole Shaping until
Top is 8[8·5,9,9·5] cm (3[3¼,
3½,3¾] in) from beginning.
Fasten off.

Collar

With 3·50 mm (No 9)
hook commence
with 50[54,58,62] ch tightly to
measure 27[29,32,34] cm (10½[11½,
12½,13½] in).
Foundation Row
As Back Foundation Row: 48[52,56,
60] – sts.
Next Row
Change to 4·00 mm (No. 8) hook, 3 ch,
1 tr into first tr, 1 tr into
each tr, 2 tr into 3rd of 3 ch,

turn: 2 – tr increased.
 Rep last row until Collar is
6[7,8,9] cm (2½[2¾,3¼,3½] in)
from beginning. Fasten off.

Join side and shoulder seams. Set
in sleeves. Join sleeve seams.
Sew collar to neck.

Neck Edging

1st Row
With 4·00 mm (No 8) hook
and with right
side facing attach yarn to base
of front opening, then work
16[19,22,26] dc evenly up front
to neck seam, (mark last dc
made), 2 dc into each row-end
along side of collar, 3 dc into
corner, then work 1 dc into
each st along collar to 2nd
corner, 3 dc into corner, 2 dc
into each row-end to neck seam,
then work 16[19,22,26] dc down
2nd side of opening, turn.
2nd Row
1 dc into first dc, (1 dc
into each dc to 2nd dc at
corner, 3 dc into next dc)
twice, 1 dc into each dc to
within marked dc, 2 ch, miss
next 2 dc, * 1 dc into each of
next 4[5,6,7] dc, 2 ch, miss
next 2 dc; rep from * once
more, 1 dc into each dc to end,
turn.
3rd Row
1 dc into first dc, * 1 dc
into each st to 2nd dc at
corner, 3 dc into next dc; rep
from * once more, 1 dc into
each dc to end, turn.
 Rep last row once more. Fasten
off.

Sleeve Edgings (both alike)

1st Round
With 3·50 mm (No 9) hook and with
right side facing attach yarn to
any ch, * 1 dc into each of
next 3 ch, miss next ch; rep
from * all round, end with 1 ss
into first dc, turn.
2nd Round
1 dc into first dc, 1 dc into
each dc, 1 ss into first dc,
turn.
 Rep last round 5 times more.
Fasten off.
Lower Edging
Rep Sleeve Edging 1st round
once, then 2nd round 3 times.
Fasten off.

Sew 3 buttons down front opening
to correspond with buttonholes. □

MOTIF WAISTCOAT

Emu Super Wash 4 ply or DK (25 g balls)

	cm	in
To Fit Chest	65[72,79,87,93,99]	25½[28¼,31,34 ,36½,39]
Length	40[44,48,52,56,60]	16 [17½,19,20½,22 ,23½]

Amount Required

4 ply

Main Colour	4[4, 5, – – –]	4 [4, 5, – – –]
1st Contrast	1[1, 1, – – –]	1 [1, 1, – – –]
2nd Contrast	2[2, 3, – – –]	2 [2, 3, – – –]

DK

Main Colour	–[– – 5, 6, 6]	– [– – 5 , 6 , 6]
1st Contrast	–[– – 1, 1, 1]	– [– – 1 , 1 , 1]
2nd Contrast	–[– – 4, 5, 5]	– [– – 4 , 5 , 5]

Aero crochet hook sizes 3·00[3·50,4·00,5·50,6·00,6·50]mm
(Nos 11[9,8,5,4,3]
6 button moulds to cover

Tension
1 motif to 6·5[7,7·5,8·5,9,
9·5]cm (2½[2¾,3,3¼,3½,3¾]in).
To check your tension make a
motif. If your motif is not the
required measurement across then
refer to Tension on page 25.

For abbreviations and sizes see
pages 24 and 25.

1st Motif

Wrap M round finger once to form
a ring.
1st Round
6 dc into commencing ring, 1 ss
into first dc. Fasten off.
2nd Round
Attach C 1 to any dc, 2 dc
into same place as join, 2 dc
into each of next 5 dc, 1 ss
into first dc. Fasten off.
3rd Round
Attach C 2 to any dc, 3 ch,
leaving last lp of each tr on
hook make 2 tr into same place
as join, yarn over hook and draw
through all lps on hook, * 3 ch,
leaving last lp of each tr on
hook make 3 tr into next dc,
yarn over hook and draw through
all lps on hook; rep from *
10 times more, 3 ch, 1 ss into
3rd of 3 ch. Fasten off.
4th Round
Attach M to any 3 ch sp, 1 dc
into same place as join, * (5 ch,
1 dc into next 3 ch sp) twice,
6 ch, 1 ss into 3rd ch from
hook (a picot formed), 3 ch,
1 dc into next sp; rep from
* omitting 1 dc at end of last
rep, 1 ss into first dc.
Fasten off.

2nd Motif

As 1st Motif until 3rd round is
completed.
4th Round
Attach M to any 3 ch sp, 1 dc
into same place as join, (5 ch,
1 dc into next 3 ch sp) twice,
3 ch, 1 dc into any picot on
1st Motif, 3 ch, 1 dc into
next sp on 2nd Motif, (2 ch,
1 dc into next 5 ch sp on 1st
Motif, 2 ch, 1 dc into next
sp on 2nd Motif) twice, 3 ch,
1 dc into next picot on 1st
Motif, 3 ch, 1 dc into next sp
on 2nd Motif, then complete as
for 1st Motif. Fasten off.
  Continue to make and join motifs
into the shape in diagram.

Join shoulder seams.

Corner Inserts (8 alike)

To round off the corners in the
armhole and neck shaping attach
M to first 5 ch lp before
corner, 3 ch, 1 dbl tr into
corner, 3 ch, 1 ss into next
5 ch lp after corner. Fasten off.

continued on page 68

Far Left The simple design of these Overtops (pattern on p. 69) means that they team well with anything from an elegant skirt to casual trousers.

Left The Child's Jumper is a popular, classic design. The pattern is on p. 63.

Below These smart peaked caps are warm and practical. The pattern is on p. 76.

Armhole Edgings (both alike)

1st Round

With right side facing attach M to shoulder seam, 2 dc into same place as join, 3 dc into each of next 4 lps, 1 dc into next motif joining, (3 dc into each of next 3 lps, 2 dc into each of next 2 lps, 3 dc into each of next 3 lps, 1 dc into next motif joining) twice, 3 dc into each of next 4 lps, 1 dc into first dc.

2nd and 3rd Rounds

Working in continuous rounds make 1 dc into each dc, 1 dc into first dc.

4th Round

* 3 ch, 1 ss into last dc made, 1 dc into each of next 3 dc; rep from * all round, 1 ss into first dc. Fasten off.

Edging

1st Round

With right side facing attach M to picot at lower right front corner, 3 dc into same place as join, ** (3 dc into each of next 4 lps, 1 dc into next motif joining) 4 times, 3 dc into each of next 4 lps, 3 dc into next corner picot, ** 3 dc into each of next 3 lps, (2 dc into each of next 2 lps, 3 dc into each of next 2 lps) 4 times, 3 dc into next corner picot, rep from ** to ** once more, (3 dc into each of next 4 lps, 1 dc into next motif joining) 10 times, 3 dc into each of next 4 lps, 1 dc into first dc.

2nd Round

3 dc into next dc, 1 dc into next dc, (3 ch, miss 3 dc, 1 dc into each of next 8 dc) 5 times, 3 ch, miss 3 dc, 1 dc into next dc, * 3 dc into next dc, 1 dc into each dc until 2nd dc at next corner is reached; rep from * twice more, end with 1 dc into first dc.

3rd Round

* 3 dc into next dc, 1 dc into each st until 2nd dc at corner is reached; rep from * 3 times more, 1 ss into first dc.
  Rep 4th round of Armhole Edging once. Fasten off.

Cover 6 button moulds (see page 32) and sew them down left front to correspond with buttonholes.

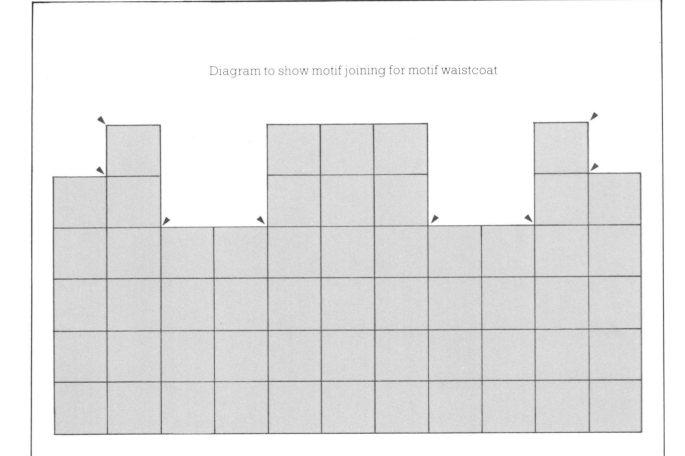

Diagram to show motif joining for motif waistcoat

▲ Corner inserts

OVERTOPS

Sirdar Wash'n'Wear DK (40 g balls), or 4 ply (20 g balls)

	cm
To Fit Chest	56[61,66,71,76,81,86,91,96,101]
Length	28[33,38,44,48,53,55,56,57, 59]

	in
To Fit Chest	22[24,26,28,30,32,34 ,36,38 ,40]
Length	11[13,15,17,19,21,21½,22,22½,23]

Amount Required	
DK	5[6, 7, 8, 9,10,11, 13,14, 16]
4 ply	6[7, 9,11,13,15,17, 19,20, 21]

Aero crochet hooks 5·00 mm and 4·00 mm (No 6 and No 8); 4·50 mm and 3·50 mm (No 7 and No 9)

Tension
DK Version – With 5·00 mm (No 6) hook 16 sts to 10 cm (4 in).
4 ply Version – With 4·50 mm (No. 7) hook 20 sts to 10 cm (4 in).
To make a tension sample commence with 17 ch (for D.K. Version) or 21 ch (for 4 ply Version) and work as Back for 15 rows. Fasten off.
If your sample is not 10 cm (4 in) across then refer to Tension on page 25.

For abbreviations and sizes see pages 24 and 25.

DK Version

Back and Front (both alike)

With 4·00 mm (No 8) hook commence with 49[53,57,63,67,71,77,81,85,89] ch to measure 31[34,36,40,42,45,48, 51,54,57] cm (12¼[13¼,14¼,15¾, 17,17¾,19¼,20¼,21¼,22¼] in).

****Foundation Row**
1 dc into 2nd ch from hook, 1 dc into each ch to end, turn.

1st Row
1 dc into first dc, * 1 tr into next dc, 1 dc into next dc; rep from * ending with 1 tr into last dc, turn.

Patt Row
1 dc into first tr, * 1 tr into next dc, 1 dc into next tr; rep from * ending with 1 tr into last dc, turn.
Rep patt row 1[1,1,2,2,2,3,3, 3,3] times more.

Next Row
Change to larger hook, 3 ch, miss first tr, * 1 tr into next dc, 1 tr into next tr; rep from * ending with 1 tr into last dc, turn.

Next Row
3 ch, miss first tr, 1 tr into each tr, 1 tr into 3rd of 3 ch, turn.
Rep last row until work is 15[19,23,27,31,35,35,35,35,35] cm (6[7½,9,10½,12,13½,13½,13½, 13½,13½] in) from beginning, **.

Shape Sleeves
Attach a 2nd thread to end of last row and make 23[26,29,32, 35,38,40,40,40,40] ch. Fasten off. With original thread make 24[27,30,33,36,39,41,41,41,41] ch.

*****1st Row**
1 dc into 2nd ch from hook, 1 dc into each ch, 1 dc into each tr, 1 dc into each ch to end, turn.
Rep patt row until work is 28[33,38,44,48,53,55,56,57,59] cm (11[13,15,17,19,21,21½,22, 22½,23] in) from beginning. Fasten off.

Join side and sleeve seams. Join shoulder seams leaving centre part unsewn to insert head. ***.

4 Ply Version

Back and Front (both alike)

With 3·50 mm (No. 9) hook commence with 61[67,73,79,83,89,95,101,105, 111] ch to measure 31[34,37,41, 43,46,49,51,54,57] cm (12¼[13½, 14¾,16,16¾,18,19¼,20¼,21¼,22½] in).
Now rep from ** to ** of DK Version once.

Shape Sleeves
Attach a 2nd thread to end of last row and make 28[32,36,40, 44,48,50,50,50,50] ch. Fasten off.
With original thread make 29[33, 37,41,45,49,51,51,51,51] ch.
Now rep from *** to *** of D.K. Version once. □

Far Right this glamorous outfit is made from a lovely soft yarn in a flattering shade of pink. The pattern for the Blouson and Skirt is on p. 77 and the pattern for the Triangular Shawl is on p. 99.

Right The Blouson can be worn with a contrasting skirt for a more casual appearance.

Left The fringing on the shawl has been used to create a dramatic effect.

Below This Bed Jacket is cleverly designed so that it is all in one piece. The pattern is on p. 81.

TABARD

Lister Tahiti (25 g balls) or Lister/Lee Target Aran (50 g balls)

	cm	in
To Fit Chest	56[61,66,71,76,81,86,91,96,101]	22[24,26,28,30,32,34,36,38,40]
Length	28[33,38,43,48,53,53,56,56, 59]	11[13,15,17,19,21,21,22,22,23]

Amount Required		
Tahiti	4[5, 6, 7, 8, 9,10,11,12, 12]	4[5, 6, 7, 8, 9,10,11,12,12]
Aran	4[5, 6, 8, 9,10,11,12,13, 14]	4[5, 6, 8, 9,10,11,12,13,14]

Aero crochet hook size 7·00 mm (No 2)

Tension
12 sts to 10 cm (4 in).
To make a tension sample
commence with 13 ch, work as
Back for 10 cm (4 in). Fasten off.
  If your sample is not 10 cm
(4 in) across then refer to
Tension on page 25.

For sizes and abbreviations
see pages 24 and 25.

Back and Front (both alike)

Working from side seam commence
with 33[39,45,51,57,63,63,66,66,
69] ch to measure 28[33,38,43,
48,53,53,56,56,69] cm (11[13,15,
17,19,21,21,22,22,23[in).
Foundation Row
1 dc into 2nd ch from hook,
1 dc into each ch to end, turn.
1st Patt Row
1 dc into first dc, 1 dc into
each dc to end, turn.
2nd Patt Row
3 ch, miss first dc, * miss
next dc, (1 tr, 1 ch, 1 tr)
into next dc, miss next dc;
rep from * ending with 1 tr
into last dc, turn: 10[12,14,
16,18,20,20,21,21,22] – 1 ch sp.
3rd Patt Row
1 dc into first tr, * 1 dc
into next tr, 1 dc into next
1 ch sp, 1 dc into next tr;
rep from * ending with 1 dc
into 3rd of 3 ch, turn.
  Rep 1st to 3rd patt rows until
work is 31[34,36,40,42,45,48,51,
54,57] cm (12¼[13½,14¼,15¾,17,
17¾,19¼,20¼,21¼,22½] in) ending
with 1st patt row. Fasten off.
  Join shoulder seams leaving
opening at neck large enough to
insert head.

Edging

With right side facing attach
yarn to lower right corner of
Front, 3 dc into same place as
join, 3 ch, 1 ss into last dc
made, * 1 dc into next dc row-
end, 2 dc into next tr row-end,
3 ch, 1 ss into last dc made,
miss next dc row-end; rep from
* across front to left corner,
3 dc into corner, ** 3 ch,
1 ss into last dc made, miss
next st, 3 dc evenly along
edge; rep from ** up side edge
to next corner, 3 ch, 1 ss into
last dc made, 3 dc into corner,
then complete to match first
side, end with 1 ss into first
dc. Fasten off.

Ties (both alike)

With 1 strand make a length of
ch 28[33,38,43,48,53,53,56,56,
59] cm (11[13,15,17,19,21,21,22,
22,23] in) long.
  Cut 6 strands of yarn and make
a tassel into end of tie (see
page 00), make another tassel
to match at other end.
  Slot the ties through the side
edges to tie under arm.

MOTHER AND DAUGHTER PONCHOS

	cm	in
Emu Mix and Match DK (25 g balls)		
Length at Centre Back	46[79]	18[31]
Main Colour	6[20]	6[20]
1st Contrast	3[6]	3[6]
2nd Contrast	1[2]	1[2]
Add an extra 2[3] balls of Main Colour for Hood		

Aero crochet hook size 4·00 mm (No 8)

Tension
16 sts and 10 rows to 10 cm
(4 in).
 To make a tension sample
commence with 16 ch, work as
Right Half for 9 rows. Fasten
off.

If your sample is not 10 cm (4 in)
across at Foundation Row then
refer to Tension on page 25.

For sizes and abbreviations
see pages 24 and 25.

Right and Left Halves (both alike)

Working from neck down with M
commence with 34[37] ch to
measure 21·5[22·5] cm (8½[9½] in).
Foundation Row
2 tr into 4th ch from hook,
* miss 2 ch, 3 tr into next
ch; rep from * to end, turn:

11[12] – 3 tr groups.
Patt Row
With M make 3 ch, 2 tr into first
tr, miss 2 tr, * 3 tr into
next sp, miss 3 tr; rep from
* ending with 3 tr into next
sp, 3 tr into 3rd of 3 ch,
turn: 1 group increased.
 Rep patt row 11[18] times more.
**1st Row
Attach C 1 to first tr, 3 ch,
2 tr into same place as join,
1 tr into each tr, 3 tr into
3rd of 3 ch. Do not turn.
2nd Row
Attach M to 3rd of 3 ch (made
at beginning of last row), 3 ch,
2 tr into same place as join,
* miss 2 tr, 3 tr into next
tr; rep from * ending with miss 2 tr,
3 tr into 3rd of 3 ch, turn.
 Rep patt row twice, 1st and
2nd row once.
7th Row
Attach C 1 to first tr, 3 ch,
2 tr into same place as join,
miss 2 tr, * 3 tr into next
sp, miss 3 tr; rep from
* ending with 3 tr into next sp,
3 tr into 3rd of 3 ch, turn.
8th Row
Attach C 2 to first tr, 3 ch,
2 tr into same place as join,
miss 2 tr, * 3 tr into next
sp, miss 3 tr; rep from
* ending with 3 tr into next
sp, 3 tr into 3rd of 3 ch. Do not turn.
9th Row
With C 1 work as patt row.
10th Row
With M work as 1st row.
11th Row
With C 1 work as 2nd row. Do not
turn.
12th Row
With C 2 work as patt row.
13th Row
With C 1 work as patt row. Do
not turn.
14th Row
With M work as patt row.
15th Row
Attach C 1 to first tr, 3 ch,
2 tr into same place as join,
* 1 tr into next tr, miss next
tr, 2 tr into next sp, miss
next tr; rep from * ending
with 1 tr into next tr, 2 tr
into 3rd of 3 ch. Do not turn.
 Rep 2nd row once and patt row
once. **
For 2nd Size Only
Rep from ** to ** once more.
For Both Sizes
Rep 1st and 2nd rows once then
rep patt row until work

continued on page 76

Below Left The Long Skirt and Waistcoat from the set on p. 84. the silver of the Victorian Blouse (pattern on p. 90) is echoed by a long black and silver skirt.

Right The attractive scalloped collar is the distinctive feature of the Jumper from the set on p. 84.

Below The pattern for the Waistcoat and Shoulder Bag can be found on p. 93.

Right The Long Cardigan (pattern on p. 82) would be ideal for gardening or other outdoor activities.

measures 36[64] cm (14[25] in)
from beginning. Fasten off.
  Join centre back and centre
front seams leaving front seam
open 8[10] cm (3[4] in) at neck.

Version with Hood

1st Row
Join M to neck edge at right
corner of front, 3 ch, 3 tr
into each of next 10[11] 2 ch sp,
3 tr into back seam, 3 tr into
each of next 10[11] 2 ch sp,
1 tr into 3rd of 3 ch, turn.

2nd Row
3 ch, 2 tr into first tr,
* miss 3 tr, 3 tr into next
sp; rep from * ending with
3 tr into 3rd of 3 ch, turn.

3rd Row
3 ch, miss first 3 tr, * 3 tr
into next sp, miss 3 tr; rep
from * ending with 3 tr into
next sp, 1 tr into 3rd of 3 ch.
  Rep last 2 rows until hood is
26[33] cm (10[13] in) from
beginning. Fasten off.
  Fold hood in half and join top seam.

Edging

Attach C 1 to base of front
opening * 2 dc into next
tr row-end, 3 ch, 1 ss into
last dc made; rep from * all
round, 1 ss into first dc.
Fasten off.

Version without Hood

Edging

Attach C 1 to base of front
opening, * 2 dc into next
tr row-end, 3 ch, 1 ss into
last dc made; rep from * up
front, then work rep into each
of next 10[11] 2 ch sp, back
seam and 10[11] 2 ch sp to next
corner, complete to match first
side, 1 ss into first dc.
Fasten off.

Both Versions

Tie

With M make a length of ch
81[91] cm (32[36] in) long, thread
this round neck to tie at front.
Make 2 bobbles (see page 32)
and attach 1 to each end.
  Cut remaining M into 20[30] cm
(8[12] in) lengths and with
3 strands make a tassel into
every alternate dc (see
page 32) round lower edge.

PEAKED CAP

Patons Pure Wool DK (25 g balls)

	cm	in
To Fit Head	50[56]	19½[22]
Amount Required	6[8]	6 [8]

Aero crochet hook size 8·00 mm and 4·00 mm (No 1 and No 8
respectively)

Tension
10 dc or first 4 Rounds to
10 cm (4 in) with 7·5 mm (No 1) hook.
To make a tension sample work the
first 4 Rounds. Fasten off.
  If your sample is not 10 cm
(4 in) across then refer to
Tension on page 25.

For abbreviations and sizes see
pages 24 and 25.

Main Section

Using 3 strands of yarn and
7·5 mm (No 1) hook wrap yarn
round finger once to form a ring.
1st Round
9 dc into commencing ring. Draw
ring tight.

2nd Round
Working in continuous
rounds throughout, 2 dc into
each of next 9 dc: 18 – dc.
3rd Round
(1 dc into each of next 2 dc,
2 dc into next dc) 6 times:
24 – dc.
4th Round
(1 dc into each of next 3 dc,
2 dc into next dc) 6 times:
30 – dc.
5th Round
(1 dc into each of next 4 dc,
2 dc into next dc) 6 times:
36 – dc.
For Largest Size Only
6th Round
(1 dc into each of next 5 dc,
2 dc into next dc) 6 times:
42 – dc.
For Both Sizes
Next Round
(2 dc into next dc, 1 tr into
next dc) 18[21] times.
Next Round
(1 dc into back lp only of each
of next 2 dc, 1 tr round back

of next tr) 18[21] times.
  Rep last round until work is 17[20] cm (7[8] in) from beginning. Break off 1 strand.

Next Round

With 2 strands and 4·00 mm (No 8) hook
make (1 dc into each of next 2 dc, 1 dc into next tr) 18[21] times.

Next Round

1 dc into each dc all round. Leave the 2 strands hanging.

Peak

With 7·5 mm hook (No 1) and right side facing attach 3 new strands to front lp only of 11th dc (counting along from hanging strands), 3 ch, 1 tr into same place as join, (1 tr into front lp only of next dc, 2 tr into front lp only of next dc) 6[8] times. Turn work round, then working into remaining lps make (2 tr into next lp, 1 tr into next lp) 6[8] times, 2 tr into last lp. Fasten off.

Last Round

Using the 2 strands left hanging and 4·00 mm (No 8) hook
make 1 dc into
each of next 8 dc, then working across double thickness of peak make (2 dc into next tr, 1 dc into next tr) 10[13] times, miss next 2 dc, 1 dc into each dc, end with 1 ss into first dc. Fasten off.

Lining

With single strand and 7·5 mm (No 1) hook, working into back lps of dc throughout, work as Main Section until 5th[6th] Round is completed.

Next Round

(1 dc into each of next 2 dc, 2 dc into next dc, 1 dc into each of next 2[3] dc, 2 dc into next dc) 6 times: 48[54] – dc.

Next Rounds

Working in continuous rounds make 1 dc into each dc until lining is 15[18] cm (6[7] in) from beginning, end with 1 ss into first dc. Fasten off.
  Insert Lining into Main Section. Sew Lining into position with a herringbone stitch.
  Make a bobble (see page 32) and sew to centre of cap.

BLOUSON AND SKIRT

Patons Kismet (50 g balls)		
	cm	in
To Fit Chest	86[91, 96,101]	34[36,38,40]
To Fit Hips	91[96,101,106]	36[38,40,42]
Blouson Length	56	22
Skirt Length	76	30
Amount Required	Skirt	Blouson
	6[7, 7, 8]	5[5, 6, 6]

Aero crochet hooks sizes 4·50 mm and 3·50 mm (Nos 7 and 9 respectively)
Waist length of elastic

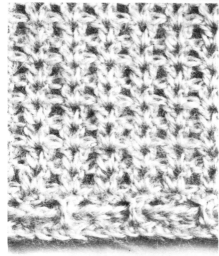

Tension
15 sts to 10 cm (4 in) with 4·50 mm (No 7) hook.
  To make a tension sample commence with 16 ch, work as Blouson Back for 14 rows. Fasten off.
  If your sample is not 10 cm (4 in) across then refer to Tension on page 25.

For sizes and abbreviations see pages 24 and 25.

Skirt

Back and Front (both alike)

With 3·50 mm (No 9) hook, working from

continued on page 80

Above The cream smock with attractive high yoke can be worn over a plain top. the pattern is on p. 88.

Left This Mohair Stole (pattern on p. 98) combines well with almost any dress for day or evening wear.

Right A collection of shawls in unusual, subtle shades. **From Left to Right:** Motif Shawl (pattern on p. 112); Semi-circular Shawl (pattern on p. 108) and the Shawl of Shells (pattern on p. 100).

waist down commence with 82[79, 86,93] ch to measure 40[39,42, 43] cm (16[15½,16½,17] in).

Foundation Row

1 dc into 2nd ch from hook, 1 dc into each ch to end, turn.

1st Row

1 dc into each dc to end, turn.
  Rep last row 4 times more: 81[78,85,92] dc.

6th Row

Change to 4·50 mm (No 7) hook, 3 ch, miss first dc, * 2 ch, miss next 3[2,2,2] dc, (4 tr, 1 ch, 4 tr) into next dc, 2 ch, miss next 3 dc, 1 tr into next dc; rep from * 9[10,11,12] times more, turn.

7th Row

3 ch, * 2 ch, (4 tr, 1 ch, 4 tr) into next 1 ch sp, 2 ch, 1 tr into next single tr; rep from * working 1 tr at end of last rep into 3rd of 5 ch, turn.
  Rep last row 7 times more.

15th Row

3 ch, * 3 ch, (4 tr, 1 ch, 4 tr) into next 1 ch sp, 3 ch, 1 tr into next single tr; rep from * working 1 tr at end of last rep into 3rd of 6 ch, turn.
  Rep last row 8 times more.

24th Row

3 ch, * 4 ch, (4 tr, 1 ch, 4 tr) into next 1 ch sp, 4 ch, 1 tr into next single tr; rep from * working 1 tr at end of last rep into 3rd of 7 ch, turn.
  Rep last row 8 times more.

33rd Row

3 ch, * 5 ch, (4 tr, 1 ch, 4 tr) into next 1 ch sp, 5 ch, 1 tr into next single tr; rep from * working 1 tr at end of last rep into 3rd of 8 ch, turn.
  Rep last row 8 times more.

42nd Row

3 ch, * 6 ch, (4 tr, 1 ch, 4 tr) into next 1 ch sp, 6 ch, 1 tr into next single tr; rep from * working 1 tr at end of last rep into 3rd of 9 ch, turn.
  Rep last row until skirt is 76 cm (30 in) from beginning. Fasten off.

Blouson

Back

With 4·50 mm (No. 7) hook commence with 76[80,84,88] ch to measure 48[51, 53,55] cm (19[20,21,22] in).
  Rep Skirt Foundation Row once.

1st Row

4 ch, miss first 2 dc, (1 tr into next dc, 1 ch, miss next

dc) 36[38,40,42] times, 1 tr into last dc, turn: 37[39,41, 43]–1 ch sp.

2nd Row

1 dc into first tr, * 1 dc into next 1 ch sp, 1 dc into next tr; rep from * ending with 1 dc into last sp, 1 dc into 3rd of 4 ch, turn.

3rd Row

3 ch, 1 tr into first dc, (miss next dc, 2 tr into next dc) 37[39,41,43] times, turn.

Patt Row

3 ch, 1 tr into first sp, * miss next sp, 2 tr into next sp; rep from * to end, turn.
  Rep last row until back is 56 cm (22 in) from beginning. Fasten off.

Front

As Back to within last 21[21,23,23] rows.

Shape Neck 1st Side

Mark sp at centre of row.

1st Row

3 ch, 1 tr into first sp, * miss next sp, 2 tr into next sp; rep from * to within marked sp, turn: 38[40,42,44]–sts.

2nd Row

1 ss into next sp, 3 ch, * miss next sp, 2 tr into next sp; rep from * to end, turn.
  Rep patt row 3 times.
  Rep last 4 rows 4 times more.

For 3rd and 4th Sizes Only

Rep 2nd row once, patt row once.

For All Sizes

Fasten off.

Shape Neck 2nd Side

1st Row

Attach yarn to first sp after marked sp, 3 ch, 1 tr into same place as join, * miss next sp, 2 tr into next sp; rep from * to end, turn.

2nd Row

3 ch, 1 tr into first sp, * miss next sp, 2 tr into next sp; rep from * to within last 2 sp, end with miss next sp, 1 tr into last sp, turn.

3rd Row

1 ss into next tr, 3 ch, 1 tr into next sp, * miss next sp, 2 tr into next sp; rep from * to end, turn.
  Rep last 4 rows 4 times more.

For 3rd and 4th Sizes Only

Rep 2nd and 3rd rows once more.

For All Sizes

Fasten off.
  Join skirt side seams. Sew elastic to waist with a herringbone casing (see page 32).

Join blouson side seams leaving top 19[20,21,22] cm (7½[8,8½,9] in) unsewn for armholes. Join shoulder seams.

Armhole Edgings (both alike)

1st Round

With 4·50 mm (No. 7) hook and right side facing attach yarn to base of armhole, make 2 dc into each row-end all round, 1 ss into first dc.

2nd Round

* 3 ch, 1 ss into last dc made, 1 dc into each of next 4 dc; rep from * omitting 1 dc at end of last rep, 1 ss into first dc. Fasten off.

Neck Edging

1st Round

With 4·50 mm (No. 7) hook and with right side facing attach yarn to base of front neck, 1 dc into same place as join, 2 dc into each row-end up right side, 1 dc into each tr across back, 2 dc into each row-end down left side, 1 dc into first dc.
  Rep 2nd Round of Armhole Edging once. Fasten off.

Tie

With 2 strands make a length of ch 100[105,110,115] cm (39[41, 43,45] in). Thread this through 1st row of blouson to tie at centre front. Make 2 bobbles (see page 32) and attach 1 to each end of tie.

BED JACKET

Templetons H and O Shetland Lace 3 ply (25 g balls)

	cm	in
Length excluding cuffs	148	58
Depth	50	20
Amount Required	7	7

Aero crochet hook size 3·50 mm (No 9)

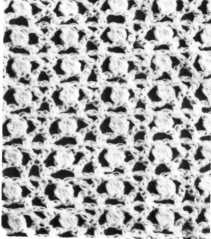

Tension
4 patt to 10 cm (4 in).
To make a tension sample
commence with 30 ch, work as
bed jacket for 11 rows. Fasten
off.
 If your sample is not 10 cm
(4 in) across then refer to
Tension on page 25.

For abbreviations and sizes see
pages 24 and 25.

To Make

Commence with 126 ch to measure
53 cm (20¾ in).
Foundation Row
(Right Side) 1 tr into 6th ch
from hook, * miss 2 ch, leaving
last lp of each tr on hook make
4 tr into next ch, yarn over
hook and draw through all lps
on hook (a cluster formed),
1 ch, miss 2 ch, (1 tr, 2 ch,
1 tr) into next ch; rep from
* to within last 6 ch, end with
miss 2 ch, leaving last lp of
each tr on hook make 4 tr into
next ch, yarn over hook and draw
through all lps on hook (another
cluster formed), 1 ch, (1 tr,
2 ch, 1 tr) into last ch,
turn: 20 – clusters.
1st Patt Row
5 ch, miss first tr, * 1 dc
into next tr, 5 ch; rep from
* ending with 3 ch, 1 tr into

3rd of 5 ch, turn.
2nd Patt Row
5 ch, 1 tr into first tr,
* a cluster into 3rd ch of next
5 ch lp, 1 ch, (1 tr, 2 ch,
1 tr) into 3rd ch of next
5 ch lp; rep from * to within
last 2 lps, end with a cluster
into 3rd ch of next 5 ch lp,
1 ch, (1 tr, 2 ch, 1 tr) into
3rd of 5 ch, turn.
 Rep 1st and 2nd patt rows until
work is 148 cm (58 in) from
beginning ending with 2nd patt
row.
Cuff
1st Row
1 dc into first tr, * 1 dc
into next 2 ch sp, 1 dc into
next cluster; rep from * ending
with 1 dc into 3rd of 5 ch,
turn: 41 – dc.
**2nd Row
3 ch, miss first dc, 1 tr
into each dc to end, turn.
3rd Row
3 ch, miss first tr, 1 tr into
each tr, 1 tr into 3rd of 3 ch,
turn.
 Rep last row 12 times more.
16th Row
* 5 ch, 1 dc into next tr;
rep from * ending with 5 ch,
1 dc into 3rd of 3 ch, 5 ch,
turn.
17th Row
* 1 dc into next 5 ch lp,
5 ch; rep from * ending with
1 dc into last 5 ch lp, 3 ch,
1 dbl tr into last dc, turn.
Last Row
* 5 ch, 1 ss into 3rd ch from
hook, 2 ch, 1 dc into next
5 ch lp; rep from * to end.
Fasten off. **.
2nd Cuff
1st Row
Working along other side of
commencing ch with wrong side
facing attach yarn to first sp,
2 dc into same place as join,
1 dc into each sp: 41 – dc.
 Rep from ** to ** of first
cuff.
 Join cuff seams.

Side Edgings (both alike)

With right side facing attach
yarn to first row-end, 2 dc
into same place as join, * 3 ch,
1 ss into last dc made, 1 dc
into each of next 2 row-ends;
rep from * to end. Fasten off.

LONG CARDIGAN

	cm	in
Patons Fiona DK (50 g balls)		
To Fit Chest	81[86,91,96]	32 [34,36 ,38]
Length	67[68,70,71]	26½[27,27½,28]
Sleeve Seam	46	18
Amount Required	9[9,10,10]	9 [9,10, 10]

5 Button Moulds
Aero crochet hook sizes 5·00 mm and 4·00 mm
(No 6 and No 8 respectively)

Tension
16 sts to 10 cm (4 in).
To make a tension sample
commence with 19 ch, work as
back for 13 rows. Fasten off.
  If your sample is not 10 cm
(4 in) across then refer to
Tension on page 25.

For sizes and abbreviations
see pages 24 and 25.

Back

With 5·00 mm (No 6) hook
commence
with 73[77,81,85] ch to measure
47[50,52,55] cm (18½[19½,20½,
21½] in).

Foundation Row
1 dc into 4th ch from hook,
* 1 tr into next ch, 1 dc into
next ch; rep from * ending with
1 tr into last ch, turn:
71[75,79,83] – sts.

1st Patt Row
3 ch, 1 dc into front lp of
next dc, 1 tr into next tr;
rep from * working 1 tr at end
of last rep into 3rd of 3 ch,
turn.

2nd Patt Row
3 ch, * 1 dc into back lp of
next dc, 1 tr into next tr;
rep from * working 1 tr at end
of last rep into 3rd of 3 ch,
turn.
  Rep last 2 rows until back is
42 cm (16½ in) from beginning
ending with 2nd patt row.

Shape Raglan

1st Row
1 ss into each of next 3 sts,
* 1 dc into front lp of next
dc, 1 tr into next tr; rep
from * to within last 4 sts, end
with 1 dc into front lp of next
dc, turn: 6 – sts decreased.

2nd Row
1 ss into next st, 3 ch,
* 1 dc into back lp of next dc,
1 tr into next tr; rep from
* to within last st, turn:
2 – sts decreased.

3rd Row
* 1 dc into front lp of next
dc, 1 tr into next tr; rep
from * to within last st, turn:
2 – sts decreased.
  Rep last 2 rows 10[11,12,13]
times more then 2nd row once:
19 – sts remain. Fasten off.

Pocket Linings (2 alike)

With 5·00 mm (No 6)
hook commence
with 21 ch to measure 12 cm
(5 in).
  Work as Back until lining is
10 cm (4 in) from beginning
ending with a 2nd patt row.
Fasten off.

Right Front

With 5·00 mm (No 6) hook commence
with 37[39,41,43] ch to measure
24[26,27,28] cm (9½[10,10½,11] in).
  Work as Back until front is

10 cm (4 in) from beginning ending with a 2nd patt row: 35[37,39,41] – sts on Foundation Row.

Insert Pocket Row

3 ch, (1 dc into front lp of next dc, 1 tr into next tr) 3[3,4,4] times, 1 dc into front lp of next dc, place pocket lining into position and work across these 19 sts with 1 tr into first tr, (1 dc into front lp of next dc, 1 tr into next tr) 8 times, 1 dc into front lp of next dc, 1 tr into 3rd of 3 ch, miss next 19 sts on front, (1 dc into front lp of next dc, 1 tr into next tr) 3[4,4,5] times, 1 dc into front lp of next dc, 1 tr into 3rd of 3 ch, turn.

Continue as Back to Shape Raglan.

Shape Raglan and Neck

1st Row

1 ss into each of first 3 sts, * 1 dc into front lp of next dc, 1 tr into next tr; rep from * to within last 2 sts, 1 dc into front lp of next dc, turn.

2nd Row

* 1 dc into back lp of next dc, 1 tr into next tr; rep from * to within last st, turn.

3rd Row

* 1 dc into front lp of next dc, 1 tr into next tr; rep from * to within last st, turn.

4th Row

3 ch, * 1 dc into back lp of next dc, 1 tr into next tr; rep from * to within last st, turn.

5th Row

* 1 dc into front lp of next dc, 1 tr into next tr; rep from * to within last 2 sts, end with 1 dc into front lp of next dc, turn.

Rep last 4 rows 3[4,4,5] times more, then 2nd row once.

For 1st and 3rd Sizes Only

Rep 3rd and 4th rows once.

For All Sizes

Next Row

3 ch, 1 tr into last st, turn.

Last Row

Make 3 ch. Fasten off.

Left Front

As Right Front to Insert Pocket Row.

Insert Pocket Row

3 ch, (1 dc into front lp of next dc, 1 tr into next tr) 3[4,4,5] times, 1 dc into front lp of next dc, place pocket lining into position and work

across these 19 sts with 1 tr into first tr, (1 dc into front lp of next dc, 1 tr into next tr) 8 times, 1 dc into front lp of next dc, 1 tr into 3rd of 3 ch, miss next 19 sts on front, (1 dc into front lp of next dc, 1 tr into next tr) 3[3,4,4] times, 1 dc into front lp of next dc, 1 tr into 3rd of 3 ch, turn.

Continue as Back to Shape Raglan.

Shape Raglan and Neck

1st Row

* 1 dc into front lp of next dc, 1 tr into next tr; rep from * to within last 4 sts, 1 dc into front lp of next dc, turn.

2nd Row

1 ss into next st, 3 ch, * 1 dc into back lp of next dc, 1 tr into next tr; rep from * ending with 1 dc into back lp of last dc, turn.

3rd Row

1 ss into next st, 3 ch, * 1 dc into front lp of next dc, 1 tr into next tr; rep from * to within last 2 sts, 1 dc into front lp of next dc, turn.

4th Row

1 ss into next st, 3 ch, * 1 dc into back lp of next dc, 1 tr into next tr; rep from * working 1 tr at end of last rep into 3rd of 3 ch, turn.

5th Row

* 1 dc into front lp of next dc, 1 tr into next tr; rep from * ending with 1 dc into front lp of next dc, turn.

Rep last 4 rows 3[4,4,5] times more, then 2nd row once.

For 1st and 3rd Sizes Only

Rep 3rd and 4th rows once.

For All Sizes

Next Row

3 ch, 1 tr into last st, turn.

Last Row

Make 3 ch. Fasten off.

Sleeves (both alike)

With 5·00 mm (No. 6) hook commence with 51[55,59,63] ch to measure 32[34,37,39] cm (12½[13½,14½,15½] in). Rep Back Foundation Row once: 49[53,57,61] – sts.

** Rep 1st and 2nd patt rows 3 times.

1st Inc Row

3 ch, (1 dc, 1 tr) into first tr, * 1 dc into front lp of next dc, 1 tr into next tr;

rep from * working 1 tr at end of last rep into 3rd of 3 ch, turn: 2 – sts increased.

Rep 2nd and 1st patt rows 3 times.

2nd Inc Row

3 ch, (1 dc, 1 tr) into first tr, * 1 dc into back lp of next dc, 1 tr into next tr; rep from * working 1 tr at end of last rep into 3rd of 3 ch, turn: 2 sts – increased. **.

Rep from ** to ** once more. Rep 1st and 2nd patt rows 3 times then 1st inc row once: 59[63,67,71] – sts.

Continue to rep patt rows without further shaping until Sleeve is 42 cm (17 in) from beginning ending with 2nd patt row.

Shape Raglan

As Back Raglan: 7 – sts remain. Fasten off.

Join raglan seams. Join side and sleeve seams. Sew in pocket linings.

Edging

1st Round

With 4·00 mm (No 8) hook and right side facing attach yarn to any ch at lower edge, 1 dc into same place as join, 1 dc into each ch to corner, 3 dc into corner, then work * 2 dc into next row-end, 1 dc into next row-end; rep from * up front, 1 dc into each st across back, work down 2nd front to match first 3 dc into corner, 1 dc into each ch, 1 ss into first dc, turn.

2nd Round

(1 dc into each dc to centre dc at corner, 3 dc into next dc) twice, 1 dc into each dc, 1 ss into first dc, turn.

1st Buttonhole Row

1 dc into each dc to centre dc at corner, 3 dc into next dc, (3 ch, miss 3 dc, 1 dc into each of next 12 dc) 4 times, 3 ch, miss 3 dc, 1 dc into each dc to centre dc at corner, 3 dc into next dc, 1 dc into each dc, 1 ss into first dc, turn.

2nd Buttonhole Row

1 dc into each dc to centre dc at corner, 3 dc into next dc, 1 dc into each dc up left front, round neck to first buttonhole (3 dc into next 3 ch lp, 1 dc into each of next

continued overleaf

12 dc) 4 times, 3 dc into next
3 ch lp, 1 dc into each dc to
centre dc at corner, 3 dc into
next dc, 1 dc into each dc,
1 ss into first dc, turn.
  Rep 2nd Round twice. Fasten off.

Cuffs (both alike)

1st Round
With 4·00 mm (No 8) hook and wrong
side facing attach yarn to any
ch, 1 dc into same place as
join, 1 dc into each of next
2 ch, miss next ch, 1 ss into
first dc, turn.

2nd Round
Make 1 dc into each dc, 1 ss
into first dc, turn.
  Rep last round 12 times more.
Fasten off.

Pocket Edgings (both alike)

1st Row
With 4·00 mm (No 8) hook and right
side facing attach yarn to first
st left free on Pocket Insert
Row, 1 dc into same place as
join, 1 dc into each of next
18 sts, turn.

2nd Row
1 dc into first dc, 1 dc into
each dc to end, turn.
  Rep last row 3 times more.
Fasten off.
  Sew sides of edging into position.

Belt

With 4·00 mm (No 8)
hook commence
with 6 ch.

Foundation Row
1 dc into 2nd ch from hook,
1 dc into each ch to end, turn.

1st Row
1 dc into first dc, 1 dc into
each dc to end, turn.
  Rep last row until belt is
100 cm (39 in) from beginning.
Fasten off.

Edging

With right side facing attach
yarn to any st, then work 1 dc
into each st and row-end all
round making 3 dc into each of
the 4 corners, end with 1 ss
into first dc. Fasten off.
  Cover 5 button moulds (see
page 32) and sew them down left
front to correspond with
buttonholes.

JUMPER, WAISTCOAT AND SKIRT

Templetons H and O Shetland Fleece 4 ply (25 g balls)

	cm	in
To Fit Bust	86[91, 96,101]	34[36 ,38,40]
To Fit Hips	91[96,101,106]	36[38 ,40,42]
Jumper Length	61[62, 63, 64]	24[24½,25,25½]
Sleeve Seam	46[46, 46, 46]	18[18 ,18,18]
Skirt Length	106[106,106,106]	42[42 ,42,42]
Waistcoat Length	66[67, 68, 69]	26[26½,27,27½]

Amount Required		
Jumper	16[17, 17, 18]	16[17 ,17,18]
Skirt	25[26, 26, 27]	25[26 ,26,27]
Waistcoat	9[9, 10, 10]	9[9 ,10,10]

Aero crochet hook sizes 3·50 mm, 4·00 mm and 4·50 mm
(Nos 9, 8 and 7 respectively)
Length of elastic for skirt to fit waist measurement
3 buttons for back opening of jumper

Tension
4 patt to 10 cm (4 in) with 4·00 mm
(No 8) hook.

To make a tension sample
commence with 23 ch, work as
Jumper Back for 12 rows. Fasten off.

If your sample is not 10 cm (4 in)
across then refer to Tension on
page 25.

For abbreviations and sizes see
pages 24 and 25.

Jumper

Back

Using 4·00[4·50,4·00,4·50] mm (No 8
[No 7,No 8,No 7]) hook and
working from lower edge up
commence with 93[93,103,103] ch to
measure 47[49,52,54] cm (18½[19½,
20½,21½] in).
Foundation Row
4 tr into 5th ch from hook,
* miss next 2 ch, 1 tr into
next ch, miss next ch, 4 tr
into next ch (a shell formed);
rep from * ending with miss next
2 ch, 1 tr into last ch, turn:
18[18,20,20] – shells.
Patt Row
3 ch, * 4 tr into centre sp
of next shell, 1 tr into next
single tr; rep from * working
1 tr at end of last rep into
3rd of 3 ch, turn.

Rep last row until Back is
41 cm (16 in) from beginning.
Shape Armholes
1st Row
Ss to next single tr, 3 ch,
* 4 tr into centre sp of next
shell, 1 tr into next single
tr; rep from * to within last
5 sts, turn.
2nd Row
Ss to centre sp of next shell,
3 ch, 1 tr into same place as
last ss, * 1 tr into next
single tr, 4 tr into centre sp
of next shell; rep from * ending
with 1 tr into next single tr,
2 tr into centre sp of last shell, turn.
3rd Row
Ss to next single tr, 3 ch,
* 4 tr into centre sp of next
shell, 1 tr into next single
tr; rep from * to within last
2 sts, turn.
For 3rd and 4th Sizes Only
Rep last 2 rows once more.
For All Sizes
Divide for Back Opening
Mark tr at centre of row.
1st Row
3 ch, * 4 tr into centre sp
of next shell, 1 tr into next

single tr; rep from * until
marked tr is worked, turn.

Rep patt row until Back is
59[60,61,62] cm (23[23½,24,24½] in)
from beginning. Fasten off.
2nd Side
1st Row
Attach yarn to marked tr, then
work patt row to end, turn.
Complete to match 1st Side.
Fasten off.

Front

As Back until Armhole Shaping
is completed.

Rep patt row until 3[4,5,5]
rows less than Back have been
worked.
Shape Neck 1st Side
1st Row
3 ch, (4 tr into centre sp
of next shell, 1 tr into next
single tr) 6 times, turn.
2nd Row
Ss to next single tr, 3 ch,
* 4 tr into centre sp of next
shell, 1 tr into next single tr;
rep from * working 1 tr at end
of last rep into 3rd of 3 ch,
turn.
3rd Row
3 ch, * 4 tr into centre sp of
next shell, 1 tr into next
single tr; rep from * to
within last shell, 2 tr into
centre sp of last shell, turn.
4th Row
3 ch, 1 tr into first tr, *
1 tr into next single tr, 4 tr
into centre sp of next shell;
rep from * ending with 1 tr
into 3rd of 3 ch, turn.
For 2nd, 3rd and 4th Sizes Only
5th Row
3 ch, * 4 tr into centre sp of
next shell, 1 tr into next single
tr; rep from * ending with
2 tr into 3rd of 3 ch.
For 3rd and 4th Sizes Only
Rep 4th row once more.
For All Sizes
Fasten off.

2nd Side of Neck
1st Row
Miss centre single tr
and attach yarn to next single
tr, 3 ch, * 4 tr into centre
sp of next shell, 1 tr into
next single tr; rep from *
working 1 tr at end of last rep
into 3rd of 3 ch, turn.
2nd Row
3 ch, * 4 tr into centre sp of
next shell, 1 tr into next
single tr; rep from * to within
last shell, turn.

3rd Row
Ss to centre sp of next shell,
3 ch, 1 tr into same place as
last ss, * 1 tr into next
single tr, 4 tr into centre sp
of next shell; rep from * ending
with 1 tr into 3rd of 3 ch,
turn.

Rep 5th row of 1st Side of Neck
once.
For 2nd, 3rd and 4th Sizes Only
Rep 4th row of 1st Side of Neck
once.
For 3rd and 4th Sizes Only
Rep 5th row of 1st Side of Neck
once.
For All Sizes
Fasten off.

Sleeves (both alike)

Using 4·00 mm (No 8) hook
commence with
53[58,63,68] ch to measure
29[30,32,34] cm (10½[11½,12½,
13½] in).
Foundation Row
As Back Foundation Row: 10[11,
12,13] – shells.

Rep patt row 4 times.
1st Inc Row
5 ch, 1 tr into first tr,
* 4 tr into centre sp of next
shell, 1 tr into next single tr;
rep from * working 1 tr at end
of last rep from 3rd of 3 ch,
turn.
2nd Inc Row
3 ch, * 4 tr into centre sp of
next shell, 1 tr into next
single tr; rep from * ending
with 4 tr into centre sp of
last shell, 1 tr into next
single tr, 4 tr into 5th of
5 ch, 1 tr into 4th of 5 ch,
turn: 1 – shell increased.

Rep patt row 5 times.

Rep last 7 rows 3 times more,
then rep patt row until Sleeve
is 43 cm (17 in) from beginning.
Shape Top
Rep Back Shape Armhole 1st row
once, then 2nd and 3rd rows 5[5,
6,6] times. Fasten off.

Join side and shoulder seams.

Collar

1st Row
With 3·50 mm (No. 9) hook
and right side
facing attach yarn to neck
corner, 1 dc into same place as
join, then work 53[56,59,62] dc
evenly round neck edge, 1 dc

continued overleaf

into 2nd corner, turn: 55[58, 61,64]–dc altogether.

2nd Row
3 ch, miss first dc, (4 tr into next dc, miss next dc, 1 tr into next dc) 18[19,20,21] times, turn.
 Rep patt row twice.
 Change to 4·50 mm (No 7) hook and rep patt row twice.

7th Row
3 ch, * 1 ch, 4 tr into centre sp of next shell, 1 ch, 1 tr into next single tr; rep from * working 1 tr at end of last rep into 3rd of 3 ch, turn.

8th Row
3 ch, * 1 ch, 4 tr into centre sp of next shell, 1 ch, 1 tr into next single tr; rep from * working 1 tr at end of last rep into 3rd of 4 ch, turn.
 Rep last row once more.

10th Row
* 1 ch, 6 tr into centre sp of next shell, 1 ch, 1 ss into next single tr; rep from * working 1 ss at end of last rep into 3rd of 4 ch. Fasten off.

Skirt

Back and Front (both alike)

With 4·00 mm (No 8) hook and working from waist down commence with 80[86,92,98] ch to measure 38[41,44,47] cm (15[16¼,17½,18¾] in).

Foundation Row
1 dc into 2nd ch from hook, 1 dc into each ch to end, turn.

1st Row
1 dc into first dc, 1 dc into each dc to end, turn.
 Rep last row 5 times more.

7th Row
3 ch, 1 tr into first dc, miss next dc, (1 tr into each of next 3 dc, miss next dc, 4 tr into next dc, miss next dc) 12[13,14,15] times, 1 tr into each of next 3 dc, miss next dc, 2 tr into last dc, turn: 12[13,14,15]–4 tr shells.

8th Row
3 ch, 1 tr into first tr, miss next tr, (1 tr into each of next 3 tr, 4 tr into centre sp of next shell, miss remaining 2 tr of shell) 12[13,14,15] times, 1 tr into each of next 3 tr, 2 tr into 3rd of 3 ch, turn.
 Rep 8th row 5 times.

14th Row
3 ch, 1 tr into first tr, miss

next tr, (2 tr into next tr, 1 tr into each tr to next shell, 4 tr into centre sp of shell, miss remaining 2 tr of shell) 12[13,14,15] times, 2 tr into next tr, 1 tr into each tr to within last 2 sts, 2 tr into 3rd of 3 ch, turn: 13[14,15,16]–tr increased.

15th Row
3 ch, 1 tr into first tr, miss next tr, * 1 tr into each tr to next shell, 4 tr into centre sp of shell, miss remaining 2 tr of shell; rep from * ending with 1 tr into each tr to within last 2 sts, 2 tr into 3rd of 3 ch, turn.
 Rep 15th row 9 times more.
 Rep last 11 rows 6 times more.
 Rep 14th row once.
 (There are 11 tr between the shells.)
 Rep 15th row until Skirt is 90 cm (36 in) from beginning.

Next Row
3 ch, 1 tr into first tr, miss next tr, (1 tr into each of next 4 tr, miss next tr, 4 tr into next tr, miss next tr, 1 tr into each of next 4 tr, 4 tr into centre sp of next shell, miss remaining 2 tr of shell) 12[13,14,15] times, 1 tr into each of next 4 tr, miss next tr, 4 tr into next tr, miss next tr, 1 tr into each of next 4 tr, 2 tr into 3rd of 3 ch, turn: 25[27,29,31]–shells.
 Rep 15th row until Skirt is 104 cm (41 in).

Last Row
3 ch, 2 tr into first tr, miss next tr, * 1 dc into each of next 4 tr, 6 tr into centre sp of shell, miss remaining 2 tr of shell; rep from * ending with 1 dc into each tr to within last 2 sts, 3 tr into 3rd of 3 ch. Fasten off.

Waistcoat

Back

With 3·50[4·00,3·50,4·00] mm (No. 9 [No 8,No 9,No 8]) hook and working from lower edge up commence with 99[99,111,111] ch to measure 47[49·5,52,53·5] cm (18½[19½,20½,21½] in).

Foundation Row
1 tr into 3rd ch from hook, miss next ch, (1 tr into each of next 4[4,5,5] ch, miss next 2 ch, 4 tr into next ch, miss next ch) 11 times, 1 tr into each of next 4[4,5,5] ch, miss

next 2 ch, 2 tr into last ch: 11–shells.
 Rep 15th row of Skirt until Back is 15 cm (6 in) from beginning.

Next Row
3 ch, 1 tr into first tr, miss next tr, * 1 tr into each of next 12[12,15,15] tr, 4 tr into centre sp of next shell, miss remaining 2 tr of shell; rep from * ending with 1 tr into each of next 12[12,15,15] tr, 2 tr into 3rd of 3 ch, turn: 5–shells.
 Rep 15th row of Skirt until Back is 44 cm (17½ in) from beginning.

Shape Armhole

1st Row
1 ss into each of next 6[6,8,8] sts, 3 ch, (1 tr into each tr to next shell, 4 tr into centre sp of shell, miss remaining 2 tr of shell) 5 times, 1 tr into each of next 8[8,9, 9] tr, turn.

2nd Row
1 ss into next st, 3 ch, * 1 tr into each tr to next shell, 4 tr into centre sp of shell, miss remaining 2 tr of shell; rep from * ending with 1 tr into each tr to within last st, turn.
 Rep last row 3 times more.

6th Row
3 ch, * 1 tr into each tr to next shell, 4 tr into centre sp of shell, miss remaining 2 tr of shell; rep from * ending with 1 tr into each tr, 1 tr into 3rd of 3 ch, turn.
 Rep last row until Back is 66[67, 68,69] cm (26[26½,27,27½] in) from beginning. Fasten off.

Right Front

With 3·50[4·00,3·50,4·00] mm hook commence with 51[51,57,57] ch to measure 25[26,27,28] cm (9¾[10¼,10¾,11¼] in).

Foundation Row
1 tr into 3rd ch from hook, miss next ch, (1 tr into each of next 4[4,5,5] ch, miss next 2 ch, 4 tr into next ch, miss next ch) 5 times, 1 tr into each of next 4[4,5,5] ch, miss next 2 ch, 2 tr into last ch: 5–shells.
 Continue as for Back to Shape Armhole.

Shape Armhole and Neck

1st Row
1 ss into each of next 6[6,8,8] sts, 3 ch, * 1 tr into each tr to next shell, 4 tr into centre sp of shell, miss remaining 2 tr of shell; rep from * ending with 1 tr into each tr to within last 2 sts, 2 tr into

3rd of 3 ch, turn.
2nd Row
3 ch, 1 tr into first tr,
miss next tr, * leaving last
lp of each tr on hook make
1 tr into each of next 2 tr,
yarn over hook and draw through
all lps on hook (a dec formed),
1 tr into each tr to next
shell, 4 tr into centre sp of
shell, miss remaining 2 tr of
shell; rep from * ending with
1 tr into each tr to within
last st, turn.
3rd Row
1 ss into next st, 3 ch, * 1 tr
into each tr to next shell,
4 tr into centre sp of next
shell, miss remaining 2 tr of
shell; rep from * ending with
1 tr into each tr to within
last 2 sts, 2 tr into 3rd of
3 ch, turn.
  Rep last 2 rows once more.
6th Row
3 ch, 1 tr into first tr, miss
next tr, * a dec over next
2 tr, 1 tr into each tr to
next shell, 4 tr into centre sp
of shell, miss remaining 2 tr
of shell; rep from * ending with
1 tr into each tr,
1 tr into 3rd of 3 ch, turn.
7th Row
3 ch, * 1 tr into each tr to
next shell, 4 tr into centre
sp of shell, miss remaining
2 tr of shell; rep from *
ending with 1 tr into each tr
to within last 2 sts, 2 tr into
3 ch, turn.
  Rep last 2 rows until there are
the same No. of rows as for Back.
Fasten off.

Left Front

As Right Front to Armhole and
Neck Shaping.
Shape Armhole and Neck
1st Row
3 ch, 1 tr into first tr,
miss next tr, * 1 tr into each
tr to next shell, 4 tr into
centre sp of shell, miss
remaining 2 tr of shell; rep
from * ending with 1 tr into each
of next 8[8,9,9] tr, turn.
2nd Row
1 ss into next st, 3 ch,
* 1 tr into each tr to next
shell, 4 tr into centre sp of
shell, miss remaining 2 tr of
shell; rep from * ending with
1 tr into each tr to within
last 4 sts, a dec over next
2 tr, 2 tr into 3rd of 3 ch,
turn.

3rd Row
3 ch, 1 tr into first tr,
miss next tr, * 1 tr into each
tr to next shell, 4 tr into
centre sp of shell, miss
remaining 2 tr of shell; rep
from * ending with 1 tr into
each tr to within last st, turn.
  Rep last 2 rows once.
6th Row
3 ch, miss first tr, * 1 tr
into each tr to next shell, 4 tr
into centre sp of shell, miss
remaining 2 tr of shell; rep
from * ending with 1 tr into
each tr to within last 4 sts,
a dec over next 2 tr, 2 tr into
3rd of 3 ch, turn.
7th Row
3 ch, 1 tr into first tr, miss
next tr, * 1 tr into each tr
to next shell, 4 tr into centre
sp of shell, miss remaining 2 tr
of shell; rep from * ending with
1 tr into each tr, 1 tr into
3rd of 3 ch, turn.
  Rep last 2 rows until work
matches Right Front. Fasten off.

Finishing

Join side seams of skirt. Sew
elastic to waist with a herringbone casing (see page 32).
Join side and shoulder seams of
waistcoat. Set in jumper sleeves.
Join sleeve seams.
Jumper Cuffs and Lower Edging
1st Round
With 3·50 mm (No 9) hook
and with wrong
side facing attach yarn to any
ch, then make * 1 dc into each
of next 2 ch, miss next ch,
1 dc into next ch, miss next
ch; rep from * ending with
1 ss into first dc, turn.
2nd Round
1 dc into each dc, 1 ss into
first dc, turn.
  Rep last round 8 times more.
Fasten off.
Jumper Back Opening Edging
1st Row
With 3·50 mm (No 9) hook
and with right
side facing attach yarn to left
corner of collar, 1 dc into
same place as join, 2 dc into
each tr row-end, to base, turn.
2nd Row
1 dc into first dc, 1 dc into
each dc to end. Fasten off.
  Work 2nd side to match but
beginning at base.
  Overlap Edgings at base and sew
into position.

Sew 3 buttons down opening and
use sp in patt for buttonholes.

Waistcoat Edging

With right side facing attach
yarn to lower corner of left
front, 3 ch, 8 tr into same
place as join, miss next ch,
* 1 dc into each of next 4[4,5,
5] ch, miss next 2 ch, 6 tr
into next ch, miss next ch; rep
from * ending with 1 dc into
each of next 4[4,5,5] ch, miss
next 2 ch, 9 tr into last ch,
then work rep evenly up front,
round neck and down other side,
join with 1 ss into 3rd of 3 ch.
Fasten off.

Armhole Edgings (both alike)

1st Round
With right side facing attach
yarn to base of armhole, 1 dc
into each st, then work 2 dc
into each row-end around armhole,
1 dc into each st, 1 dc into
first dc.
2nd and 3rd Rounds
Working in continuous rounds make
1 dc into each dc, end last
round with 1 ss into next dc.
Fasten off. □

SMOCK

Emu Easy-Care 4 ply (20 g balls)

	cm	in
To Fit Chest	86[94,102]	34[37,40]
Length	76	30
Sleeve Seam	42	16½
Amount Required	17[18, 19]	17[18,19]

Aero crochet hook size 3·50 mm (No 9)
1 button

Tension
20 tr to 10 cm (4 in).
To make a tension sample commence
with 22 ch, work Back Foundation
Row once. *Next row* 3 ch, miss
first tr, 1 tr into each tr,
1 tr into 3rd of 3 ch, turn.
   Rep last row 10 times more.
Fasten off.
   If your sample is not 10 cm
(4 in) across then refer to
Tension on page 25.

For sizes and abbreviations
see pages 24 and 25.

Back

Working from below armholes up
commence with 93[99,105] ch to
measure 46[50,54] cm (18¼[19¾,
21¼] in).

Foundation Row
1 tr into 4th ch from hook,
1 tr into each ch to end, turn.

Shape Armholes

1st Row
Miss first st, 1 ss into each
of next 7[9,9] sts, 3 ch, 1 tr
into each tr to within last 7[9,
9] sts, turn.

2nd Row
Miss first st, 1 ss into each
of next 2 sts, 4 ch, * miss
next tr, 1 tr into next tr,
1 ch; rep from * to within last
4 sts, miss next tr, 1 tr into
next tr, turn.

3rd Row
Miss first st, 1 ss into each
of next 2 sts, 3 ch, 1 tr into
same place as ss, * 1 tr into
next 1 ch sp, 1 tr into next
tr; rep from * to within last
sp formed by turning ch, turn.

4th Row
Miss first st, 1 ss into each
of next 2 sts, 3 ch, 1 tr into
each of next 7[8,9] sts, * 2 ch,
miss next 2 tr, 1 tr into each
of next 10[10,11] tr; rep from
* 3 times more, end with 2 ch,
miss next 2 tr, 1 tr into each
of last 8[9,10] tr, turn.

5th Row
Miss first st, 1 ss into each
of next 2 sts, 3 ch, 1 tr into
each of next 2[3,4] tr, * 2 ch,
miss next 2 tr, 1 tr into next
tr, 2 tr into next 2 ch sp,
1 tr into next tr, 2 ch, miss
next 2 tr, 1 tr into each of
next 4[4,5] tr; rep from *
3 times more, end with 2 ch,
miss next 2 tr, 1 tr into next
tr, 2 tr into next 2 ch sp,
1 tr into next tr, 2 ch, miss
next 2 tr, 1 tr into each of
next 3[4,5] tr, turn.

6th Row
3 ch, miss first tr, 1 tr
into each of next 2[3,4] tr, * 2 tr
into next 2 ch sp, 1 tr into
next tr, 2 ch, miss next 2 tr,
1 tr into next tr, 2 tr into
next 2[2,3] ch sp, 1 tr into each of
next 2 tr; rep from * ending
with 1 tr into each of next 0[1,
2] tr, 1 tr into 3rd of 3 ch,
turn.

7th Row
3 ch, miss first tr, * 1 tr
into each tr, 2 tr into next
2 ch sp; rep from * ending with

1 tr into each tr, 1 tr into 3rd of 3 ch, turn: 62[64,70]–sts.

Back Opening 1st Side
Mark 2 tr at centre of row.

1st Row

3 ch, miss first tr, 1 tr into each tr to within first marked tr, turn.

**2nd Row

3 ch, miss first tr, 1 tr into each st to end, turn.

Rep last row until armholes are 18[20,22]cm (7¼[8,8¾]in) from beginning. Fasten off. **.

Back Opening 2nd Side
1st Row

Miss 2 marked tr, attach yarn to next tr, 3 ch, 1 tr into each tr, 1 tr into 3rd of 3 ch, turn.

Rep from ** to ** of 1st Side once.

Skirt

Foundation Row

Working along other side of commencing ch with right side facing attach yarn to first ch, 1 dc into same place as join, * 2 ch, miss next 2 ch, (1 tr, 2 ch, 1 tr) into next ch, 2 ch, miss next 2 ch, 1 dc into next ch; rep from * to end, turn: 15[16,17]–patt.

1st Patt Row

1 dc into first dc, * 2 tr into next 2 ch sp, 1 tr into next tr, 4 tr into next 2 ch sp, 1 tr into next tr, 2 tr into next 2 ch sp, 1 dc into next dc; rep from * to end, turn.

2nd Patt Row

Miss first st, 1 ss into each of next 3 sts, 6 ch, * miss next 2 tr, 1 dc into next sp between tr, 3 ch, miss next 2 tr, 1 tr into next tr, miss next 4 tr, 1 tr into next tr, 3 ch; rep from * ending with miss next 2 tr, 1 dc into next sp between tr, 3 ch, miss next 2 tr, 1 tr into next tr, miss last 3 tr, turn.

3rd Patt Row

5 ch, 1 tr into first tr, * 2 ch, 1 dc into next dc, (2 ch, 1 tr into next tr) twice; rep from * ending with 2 ch, 1 dc into last dc, 2 ch, 1 tr into 3rd of 6 ch, 1 ch, 1 dbl tr into same place as last tr, turn.

4th Patt Row

3 ch, 1 tr into next 1 ch sp, * 1 tr into next tr, 2 tr into next 2 ch sp, 1 dc into next dc, 2 tr into next 2 ch sp, 1 tr into next tr, 4 tr into next 2 ch sp; rep from * ending with 1 tr into next tr, 2 tr into next 2 ch sp, 1 dc into last dc, 2 tr into last 2 ch sp, 1 tr into next tr, 1 tr into last 1 ch sp, 1 tr into 4th of 5 ch, turn.

5th Patt Row

1 dc into first tr, 3 ch, miss next tr, * 1 tr into next tr, miss next 4 tr, 1 tr into next tr, 3 ch, miss next 2 tr, 1 dc into next sp between tr, miss next 2 tr, 3 ch; rep from * ending with 1 tr into next tr, miss next 4 tr, 1 tr into next tr, 3 ch, miss next tr, 1 dc into 3rd of 3 ch, turn.

6th Patt Row

1 dc into first dc, * (2 ch, 1 tr into next tr) twice, 2 ch, 1 dc into next dc; rep from * to end, turn.

Rep 1st to 6th patt rows until Back measures 76 cm (30 in) from shoulder ending with 1st or 4th patt row. Fasten off.

Front

As Back until 7th row is completed.

Shape Neck 1st Side
1st Row

3 ch, miss first tr, 1 tr into each of next 15[16,17] tr, turn.

2nd Row

Miss first st, 1 ss into each of next 2 sts, 3 ch, 1 tr into each tr, 1 tr into 3rd of 3 ch, turn.

3rd Row

3 ch, miss first tr, 1 tr into each tr to within last 2 sts, turn.

Rep 2nd row once, then rep from ** to ** of Back once.

Shape Neck 2nd Side
1st Row

Attach yarn to 16th[17th,18th] st counting from other edge, 3 ch, 1 tr into each tr, 1 tr into 3rd of 3 ch, turn.

Rep 3rd, 2nd and 3rd rows of Shape Neck 1st Side once.

Rep from ** to ** of Back once.

Skirt

As Back Skirt.

Sleeves (both alike)

Working from below armhole up commence with 63[69,75] ch to measure 31[34,37] cm (12¼[13½, 14¼]in).

Rep Back Foundation Row once: 61[67,73]–sts.

Shape Top
1st and 2nd Rows

As 1st and 2nd Row of Back Shape Armholes.

3rd Row

3 ch, 1 tr into first tr, * 1 tr into next 1 ch sp, 1 tr into next tr; rep from * to end working 1 tr at end of last rep into 3rd of 4 ch, turn: 44[46,52]–sts.

4th Row

3 ch, miss first tr, 1 tr into each of next 8[8,9] sts, 2 ch, miss next 2 sts, * 1 tr into each of next 10[11,13] sts, 2 ch, miss next 2 tr; rep from * once more, end with 1 tr into each of next 9[9,10] sts, turn.

5th Row

Miss first st, 1 ss into each of next 2 sts, 3 ch, 1 tr into each of next 3[3,4] sts, 2 ch, miss next 2 tr, 1 tr into next tr, * 2 tr into next 2 ch sp, 1 tr into next tr, 2 ch, miss next 2 tr, 1 tr into each of next 4[5,7] tr, 2 ch, miss next 2 tr, 1 tr into next tr; rep from * once more, end with 2 tr into next 2 ch sp, 1 tr into next tr, 2 ch, miss next 2 tr, 1 tr into each of next 4[4,5] tr, turn.

6th Row

Miss first st, 1 ss into each of next 2 sts, 3 ch, 1 tr into next 1[1,2] tr, 2 tr into next 2 ch sp, 1 tr into next tr, 2 ch, * miss next 2 tr, 1 tr into next tr, 2 tr into next 2 ch sp, 1 tr into each of next 4[5,7] tr, 2 tr into next 2 ch sp, 1 tr into next tr, 2 ch; rep from * once more, end with miss next 2 tr, 1 tr into next tr, 2 tr into next 2 ch sp, 1 tr into each of next 2[2,3] tr, turn.

7th Row

Miss first st, 1 ss into each of next 2 sts, 3 ch, * 1 tr into each tr, 2 tr into next 2 ch sp; rep from * ending with 1 tr into each tr to within last 2 sts, turn.

8th Row

Miss first st, 1 ss into each of next 2 sts, 3 ch, 1 tr into each tr to within last 2 sts, turn.

Rep 8th row 2[3,4] times more.

continued overleaf

Fasten off.
Lower Section
Work as for Back Skirt until
sleeve is 42 cm (16½ in) from
underarm: 10[11,12] – patt on
Foundation Row.
  Join side and shoulder seams. Set
in sleeves. Join sleeve seams.

Neck Edging

With right side facing attach
yarn to top corner of back
opening, 3 ch, * 1 ch, 1 tr
into neck edge; rep from *
* 52[55,58] times more working
1 tr at end of last rep into
2nd corner. Fasten off.

Back Opening and Neck Edging

1st Row
With right side facing attach
yarn to base of back opening,
2 dc into each row-end up side,
3 dc into corner, * 1 dc into
next 1 ch sp, 1 dc into next
tr; rep from * round neck,
3 dc into corner, 2 dc into
each row-end down to join, turn.
2nd Row
1 dc into first dc, * 3 ch,
1 ss into last dc made, 1 dc
into each of next 3 sts; rep
from * to end. Fasten off.
  Overlap edging at base of
opening and sew into position.
Sew button to top of back and use
sp at neck as buttonhole.

VICTORIAN BLOUSE

Twilleys Goldfingering (25 g balls)		
	cm	in
To Fit Chest	86[91,96,101]	34[36,38,40]
Length	62	24½
Sleeve Seam	44	17½
Amount Required	17[18,18, 19]	17[18,18,19]

Aero crochet hook size 2·50 mm (No 12)
5 button moulds to cover

Tension
27 sts to 10 cm (4 in).
To make a tension sample
commence with 30 ch, work as
back for 13 rows. Fasten off.
  If your sample is not 10 cm
(4 in) across then refer to
Tension on page 25.

For sizes and abbreviations see
pages 24 and 25.

Back

Commence with 129[135,141,147] ch
to measure 46[48,51,53] cm
(18[19,20,21] in).

Foundation Row

1 tr into 6th ch from hook,
* 1 tr into next ch, 1 ch,
miss next ch, 1 tr into next
ch; rep from * to end, turn:
41[43,45,47]−2 tr groups.

Patt Row

4 ch, miss first tr, * 1 tr
into each of next 2 tr, 1 ch;
rep from * ending with 1 tr
into 3rd of 4 ch, turn.
  Rep patt row until Back is
44[43,42,41]cm (17½[17,16½,16]
in) from beginning.

Shape Armholes

1st Row

Miss first st, 1 ss into each
of next 6[9,9,12] sts, 4 ch,
* 1 tr into each of next 2 tr,
1 ch; rep from * to within last
2[3,3,4] 2 tr groups, 1 tr into
next tr, turn.

2nd Row

As patt row.

3rd Row

Miss first st, 1 ss into each
of next 3 sts, 4 ch, then work
rep of patt row to within last
two 1 ch sp, end with 1 tr into
next tr, turn.
  Rep last 2 rows twice more.
  Rep patt row until armholes are
18[19,20,21]cm (7[7½,8,8½]in)
from beginning. Fasten off.

Front

As Back to within 2 rows of Shape
Armholes.

Next Row

4 ch, miss first tr, (1 tr
into each of next 2 tr, 1 ch)
7[8,9,10] times, (1 tr into each
of next 2 tr, 1 tr into next
1 ch sp) 26 times, 1 tr into
each of next 2 tr, * 1 ch,
1 tr into each of next 2 tr;
rep from * ending with 1 ch,
1 tr into 3rd of 4 ch, turn.

Next Row

4 ch, miss first tr, (1 tr
into each of next 2 tr, 1 ch)
7[8,9,10] times, 1 tr into each
of next 3 tr, * 2 ch, miss
2 tr, 1 tr into next tr; rep
from * 24 times more, 1 tr into
each of next 2 tr, 1 ch, then
work rep and ending of patt
row, turn.

Front Opening and Shape Armhole

1st Row

Miss first st, 1 ss into each
of next 6[9,9,12] sts, 4 ch,
(1 tr into each of next 2 tr,
1 ch) 5[5,6,6] times, 1 tr into
each of next 3 tr, 2 ch, (1 tr
into next tr, 2 tr into next
2 ch sp) 23 times, 1 tr into

next tr, 2 ch, 1 tr into each
of next 3 tr, 1 ch, then work
rep and ending of Back Armhole
Shaping 1st Row, turn.

2nd Row

4 ch, miss first tr, (1 tr
into each of next 2 tr, 1 ch)
5[5,6,6] times, 1 tr into each
of next 3 tr, 2 ch, 1 tr into
each of next 3 tr, * 1 ch, miss
2 tr, 1 tr into next tr, 1 ch,
miss 2 tr, 5 tr into next tr
(a shell made); rep from *
4 times more, end with 1 ch, miss
2 tr, 1 tr into next tr, turn.
Mark where last tr was worked.

3rd Row

3 ch, 2 tr into first tr,
* 1 ch, 1 tr into centre tr of
next shell, 1 ch, 5 tr into
next single tr; rep from *
ending with 1 ch, 1 tr into
each of next 3 tr, 2 ch, 1 tr
into each of next 3 tr, 1 ch,
then work rep and ending of Back
Armhole Shaping 3rd Row, turn.

4th Row

4 ch, miss first tr, * 1 tr
into each of next 2 tr, 1 ch;
rep from * to insert, 1 tr into
each of next 3 tr, 2 ch, 1 tr
into each of next 3 tr, ** 1 ch,
1 tr into centre tr of next
shell, 1 ch, 5 tr into next
single tr; rep from ** 4 times
more, end with 1 ch, 1 tr into
3rd of 3 ch, turn.
  Rep 3rd and 4th rows twice more.

9th Row

3 ch, 2 tr into first tr,
* 1 ch, 1 tr into centre tr of
next shell, 1 ch, 5 tr into
next single tr; rep from *
ending with 1 ch, 1 tr into
each of next 3 tr, 2 ch, 1 tr
into each of next 3 tr, 1 ch,
then work rep and ending of patt
row, turn.
  Rep 4th and 9th rows until
armhole is 14[15,16,17]cm
(5½[6,6½,7]in) from beginning
ending with 4th row. Fasten off.

Shape Neck

1st Row

Miss first 2 shells and attach
yarn to next single tr, 3 ch,
2 tr into same place as join,
then work rep and ending of
9th row, turn.

2nd Row

As 4th row to first ** ending
with 1 ch, 1 tr into centre tr
of next shell, 1 ch, 5 tr into
next single tr, 1 ch, 1 tr
into centre tr of next shell,
1 ch, 3 tr into next single
tr, turn.
  Continue in patt on these sts

until 1 more row is completed
as for back. Fasten off.

2nd Side of Front

1st Row

Attach yarn to marked st, 4 ch,
* miss 2 tr, 5 tr into next tr,
miss 2 tr, 1 ch, 1 tr into
next tr, 1 ch; rep from *
4 times more, end with miss next
tr, 1 tr into each of next
3 tr, 2 ch, 1 tr into each of
next 3 tr, 1 ch, then work rep
and ending of patt row, turn.

2nd Row

Miss first st, 1 ss into each
of next 3 sts, 4 ch, then work
rep of patt row ending with
1 tr into each of next 3 tr,
2 ch, 1 tr into each of next
3 tr, 1 ch, * 5 tr into next
single tr, 1 ch, 1 tr into
centre tr of next shell,
1 ch; rep from * 3 tr into 3rd
of 4 ch, turn.

3rd Row

4 ch, * 5 tr into next single
tr, 1 ch, 1 tr into centre tr
of next shell, 1 ch; rep from
* 1 tr into each of next 3 tr,
2 ch, 1 tr into each of next
3 tr, 1 ch, then work rep and
ending of patt row, turn.
  Rep 2nd and 3rd rows twice more.

8th Row

4 ch, miss first tr, then work
rep of patt row and ending of
2nd row, turn.
  Rep 3rd and 8th rows until there
are the same No. of rows as for
first side to Shape Neck.

Shape Neck

1st Row

4 ch, miss first tr, then work
rep of patt row ending with
1 tr into each of next 3 tr,
2 ch, 1 tr into each of next
3 tr, (1 ch, 5 tr into next
single tr, 1 ch, 1 tr into
centre tr of next shell) 3 times,
1 ch, 3 tr into next single
tr, turn.

2nd Row

Miss first st, 1 ss into each
of next 12 sts, 3 ch, 2 tr
into same place as last ss,
1 ch, 1 tr into centre tr of
next shell, 1 ch, 5 tr into
next single tr, 1 ch, 1 tr
into centre tr of next shell,
1 ch, 1 tr into each of next
3 tr, 2 ch, 1 tr into each of
next 3 tr, 1 ch, then work rep

continued overleaf

and ending of patt row, turn.
Complete as first side. Fasten off.

Sleeves (both alike)

Commence with 63[63,75,75] ch
to measure 24[24,27,27]cm
(9½[9½,10½,10½]in).

Foundation Row
1 tr into 4th ch from hook,
1 tr into each ch to end, turn.

1st Row
5 ch, miss first 3 tr, * 1 tr
into next tr, 2 ch, miss 2 tr;
rep from * ending with 1 tr
into 3rd of 3 ch, turn: 20[20,
24,24]—2 ch sp

2nd Row
3 ch, * 2 tr into next 2 ch sp,
1 tr into next tr; rep from
* working 1 tr at end of last
rep into 3rd of 5 ch, turn.

3rd Row
4 ch, miss first tr, * miss
next tr, 1 tr into each of next
2 tr, 1 ch; rep from * ending
with miss next tr, 1 tr into
3rd of 3 ch, turn.
 Rep patt row 4 times.

Inc Row
4 ch, 2 tr into first tr,
* 1 ch, 1 tr into each of next
2 tr; rep from * ending with
1 ch, (2 tr, 1 ch, 1 tr) into
3rd of 4 ch, turn.
 Rep last 5 rows 2[3,3,4] times
more, then rep patt row until
Sleeve is 35 cm (13¾in).

Shape Top
Rep Back Armhole Shaping 1st row
once, then rep 2nd and 3rd rows
until top is 10[10,11,11]cm
(4[4,4½,4½]in) from beginning.
Fasten off.

Cuff

1st Row
With right side facing, working
along other side of commencing
ch attach yarn to first ch,
3 ch, 2 tr into same place as
join, * 1 ch, miss next ch,
1 tr into next ch, 1 ch, miss
next ch, 5 tr into next ch;
rep from * ending with 1 ch,
miss next ch, 1 tr into next
tr, 1 ch, miss next ch, 3 tr
into last ch, turn.

2nd Row
3 ch, * 1 ch, 5 tr into next
single tr, 1 ch, 1 tr into
centre tr of next shell; rep
from * working 1 tr at end of
last rep into 3rd of 3 ch, turn.

3rd Row
3 ch, 2 tr into first tr,
* 1 ch, 1 tr into centre tr of
next shell, 1 ch, 5 tr into
next single tr; rep from *
ending with 1 ch, 1 tr into
centre tr of next shell, 1 ch,
3 tr into 3rd of 4 ch, turn.
 Rep last 2 rows until Cuff is
9 cm (3¾in). Fasten off.
 Join side and shoulder seams. Set
in sleeves. Join sleeve seams.

Neck Band

1st Row
With right side facing attach
yarn to corner of right front,
1 dc into same place as join,
work 84[84,96,96] dc evenly
round neck edge to 2nd corner,
turn.

2nd Row
1 dc into each dc, turn.

3rd Row
5 ch, miss first 3 dc, * 1 tr
into next dc, 2 ch, miss 2 dc;
rep from * ending with 1 tr
into last dc, turn.

4th Row
1 dc into first tr, * 2 dc
into next 2 ch sp, 1 dc into
next tr; rep from * working
1 dc at end of last rep into
3rd of 5 ch, turn.
 Rep 2nd row once.

6th Row
3 ch, 2 tr into first dc,
* 1 ch, miss next dc, 1 tr
into next dc, 1 ch, miss next
dc, 5 tr into next dc; rep
from * ending with 1 ch, miss
next dc, 1 tr into next dc,
miss next dc, 1 ch, 3 tr into
last dc, turn.
 Rep Cuff 2nd row once. Fasten
off.

Right Front Edging

1st Row
With wrong side facing attach
yarn to top of front opening
then work 2 dc into each row-end
along edge, turn.

2nd Row
1 dc into first dc, * 3 ch,
1 ss into last dc made,
miss next dc, 1 dc into next
dc; rep from * to end.
Fasten off.

Left Front Edging

As Right Front Edging but
attaching yarn to base of
opening.

Front Insert Edging

With right side facing attach

yarn to last tr of insert at
shoulder seam, 2 dc into same
place as join, * 3 ch, 1 ss
into last dc made, 2 dc into
next tr on following row; rep
from * down side of insert, then
working across front make
** 3 ch, 1 ss into last dc
made, 1 dc into each of next
2 tr, miss next tr; rep from
** then work up 2nd side to other
shoulder seam to match first
side. Fasten off.
 Cover 5 button moulds (see
page 32) and sew these down
left front using sp in patt
as buttonholes.

WAISTCOAT AND SHOULDER BAG

Jaeger Match Maker Superwash DK Wool (50 g balls)

	Waistcoat				Bag	
	cm		in		cm	in
To Fit Chest	81[86,91,96]		32 [34,36 ,38]		34 × 27	13½ × 11
Length	55[56,57,58]		21½[22,22½,23]			
Main Colour 3	4[5, 5, 5]		4 [5, 5, 5]		3	3
1st Contrast 1	2[2, 2, 2]		2 [2, 2, 2]		1	1
2nd Contrast 1	1[1, 1, 1]		1 [1, 1, 1]		1	1
3rd Contrast 2	1[1, 1, 1]		1 [1, 1, 1]		2	2

6 Button Moulds
Aero crochet hook sizes 5·00 mm and 4·00 mm
(No 6 and No 8 respectively)

Tension
16 sts to 10 cm (4 in) with
5·00 mm (No 6) hook.
To make a tension sample
commence with 18 ch, work as
back for 14 rows. Fasten off.
 If your sample is not 10 cm
(4 in) across then refer to
Tension on page 25.

For abbreviations and sizes see
pages 24 and 25.

Waistcoat

Back

With 5·00 mm (No 6) hook and M
commence with 70[74,78,82] ch
to measure 45[47,50,52] cm
(17½[18½,19½,20½] in).
Foundation Row
(Wrong side is facing as this
row is worked.) 1 tr into 4th
ch from hook, 1 tr into each
ch to end, turn: 68[72,76,
80] – sts.
1st Patt Row
3 ch, miss first tr, 1 tr into
each tr to end, turn. Do not
fasten off.
2nd Patt Row
Use C 2, C 1, C 2, C 3 in
rotation each time this row is
worked. Attach Contrast yarn
to first tr, 1 dc into same
place as join, 1 dc into each
tr, 1 dc into 3rd of 3 ch.
Fasten off. Do not turn.
3rd Patt Row
Attach M to first dc made on
previous row, 3 ch, 1 tr into
each dc to end, turn.
 Rep last 3 rows until Back is
34 cm (13½ in) from beginning
ending with 3rd patt row.
Shape Armholes
1st Row
1 ss into each of next 4[5,5,
6] sts, 3 ch, 1 tr into each
tr to within last 4[5,5,6] sts,
turn. Do not fasten off.
 Rep 2nd patt row once.
3rd Row
Miss first dc, attach M to next
dc, 3 ch, 1 tr into each dc
to within last dc, turn.
4th Row
1 ss into next st, 3 ch, 1 tr
into each tr to within turning
ch, turn. Do not fasten off.
 Rep last 3 rows once more.
Continue in patt without further
shaping until Back is 52[53,55,
56] cm (20½[21,21½,22] in) from
beginning ending with 3rd patt
row. Fasten off.

Right Front

With 5·00 mm (No 6) hook and M
commence with 36[38,40,42] ch
to measure 23[24,25·5,26·5] cm
(9[9½,10,10½] in).
Foundation Row
As Back Foundation Row: 34[36,38,
40] – sts.
 Rep 1st to 3rd patt rows until
6 rows less than Back are

continued overleaf

completed to Armhole Shaping.
Shape Neck
1st Row (Mark this row)
1 ss into next st, 3 ch, 1 tr
into each tr, 1 tr into 3rd of
3 ch, turn. Do not fasten off.
Rep 2nd patt row once.
3rd Row
Attach M to first dc, 3 ch,
1 tr into each dc to within
last dc, turn.
Rep last 3 rows once more.
Shape Armhole
1st Row
1 ss into next st, 3 ch, 1 tr
into each tr to within last
4[5,5,6] sts, turn.
Rep (2nd patt row once, 3rd and
4th Back Armhole Shaping rows
once) twice.
Rep 2nd patt row once, 3rd and
1st Neck Shaping rows once.
Continue in patt without further
shaping until same No. of rows
are completed as for Back.
Fasten off.

Left Front

As Right Front to Neck Shaping.
Shape Neck
1st Row
3 ch, miss first tr, 1 tr into
each tr to within turning ch,
turn. Do not fasten off.
Rep 2nd patt row once.
3rd Row
Miss first dc, attach M to next
dc, 3 ch, 1 tr into each dc
to end, turn.
Rep last 3 rows once more.
Shape Armhole
1st Row
1 ss into each of next 4[5,5,
6] sts, 3 ch, 1 tr into each
tr to within turning ch, turn.
Rep (2nd patt row once, 3rd and
4th Back Armhole Shaping rows
once) twice.
Rep 2nd patt row once, 3rd and
1st Neck Shaping rows once.
Complete as for Right Front.

Join side and shoulder seams.

Edging

1st Round
With 4·00 mm (No. 8) hook
and with right
side facing attach C 1 to ch at
centre of lower edge, * 1 dc
into each of next 3 ch, miss
next ch; rep from * to corner,
3 dc into corner (mark last dc
just worked), ** 2 dc into each
of next 2 tr row-ends, 1 dc
into next dc row-end; rep from

** up front, 2 dc into last
tr row-end, *** 1 dc into each
of next 2 tr, miss next tr;
rep from *** across back,
complete to match first side,
end with 1 dc into first dc.
2nd Round
To place buttonholes mark first
dc worked into marked row. Mark
4 more dc evenly placed between
the 2 marked dc, 1 dc into each dc to
within 1 dc before first marked dc,
3 dc into next dc, (3 ch, miss 3 dc,
1 dc into each dc to within next
marked dc) 5 times, 3 ch, miss 3 dc,
1 dc into each dc to within 2nd dc at
next corner, 3 dc into next dc, 1 dc
into each dc, 1 dc into first dc.
3rd Round
* 1 dc into each dc to within
2nd dc at next corner, 3 dc
into next dc, 1 dc into each
st; rep from * once more, 1 dc
into first dc.
Rep last round once more, end
with 1 ss into first dc.
Fasten off.

Armhole Edgings (both alike)

1st Round
With 4·00 mm (No. 8) hook
and right side
facing attach C 1 to side seam,
1 dc into each tr, * 2 dc into
next tr row-end, 1 dc into next
dc row-end, 2 dc into next tr
row-end; rep from * ending with
1 dc into each tr, 1 dc into first dc.
2nd to 4th Rounds
Working in continuous rounds make
1 dc into each dc, end last
round with 1 ss into first dc.
Fasten off.
Cover 6 button moulds (see
page 00) and sew them down left
front to correspond with buttonholes.

Shoulder Bag

Main Section

With 5·00 mm (No 6) hook and M
commence with 106 ch to measure
68 cm (26½ in).
Foundation Row
As Back Foundation Row of
Waistcoat: 104 sts.
Rep 1st to 3rd patt rows until
work is 28 cm (11 in) from
beginning ending with 3rd patt
row. Fasten off.
Fold work in half and join side seams.

Top Edging

With 5·00 mm (No 6) hook
and right side

facing attach M to side seam,
* 2 dc into each of next 2 tr
row-ends, 1 dc into next dc
row-end; rep from * all round,
end with 1 dc into first dc.
Rep 2nd to 4th Rounds of Armhole
Edging of Waistcoat once. Fasten off.

Strap

With 8 thicknesses of C 3 make
a length of chain 168 cm (66 in)
and sew this to side seams of
bag to form a strap over shoulder.
Cut remaining contrast colour
yarn into 23 cm (9 in) lengths
then with 8 strands make a tassel
(see page 32) into each
2nd patt row across lower edge
in the appropriate colour.
Make a tassel with C 1 into
both lower corners.   □

PULL-ON AND SCARF

Jaeger Naturgarn (100 g skeins)		
UPull-on	to fit an average head	
Scarf	160 × 20 cm	63 × 8 in
Main Colour	6	6
Contrast	1	1

Aero crochet hook size 8·00 mm (No 00)

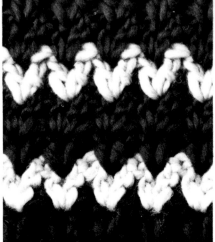

Tension
10 tr to 10 cm (4 in).
To make a tension sample
commence with 11 ch, work as
Pull-On for 9 rows. Fasten off.
If your sample is not 10 cm
(4 in) across then refer to
Tension on page 25.

For abbreviations see page 25.

Pull-On

Working from brim up with M
commence with 57 ch to measure
55 cm (21½ in).

Foundation Row
1 tr into 3rd ch from hook,
* miss next ch, 2 tr into next
ch; rep from * to end:
28 – V sts.

1st Row
With M, 3 ch, 1 tr into next
sp, * miss next sp, 2 tr into
next sp; rep from * to end,
turn.
Rep 1st row twice more. Fasten
off and turn.

**4th Row
Attach C to first tr, 3 ch,
1 tr into next sp, * miss next
sp, 2 tr into next sp; rep
from * to end. Fasten off and
turn.

5th Row
Attach M to 3rd of 3 ch made
at beginning of last row, 3 ch,
1 tr into next sp, * miss next
sp, 2 tr into next sp; rep
from * to end, turn.
Rep 1st row once. Fasten off and
turn.
Rep 4th and 5th rows once. **.
Rep 1st row until work is 34 cm
(13½ in) from beginning.

Last Row
1 ss into next sp, 3 ch, miss
next sp between tr, * 1 tr
into next sp, miss next sp;
rep from * ending with 1 tr
into last sp. Fasten off leaving
a long thread hanging.
Thread this through the top of
last row, draw tight and secure.
Now join side seam with this
thread.
Fold Brim over twice.

Scarf

With M commence with 25 ch to
measure 21 cm (10½ in).
Work Foundation Row of Pull-On
once: 12 – V sts.
Rep 1st row 5 times, then rep
from ** to ** of Pull-On once.
Rep 1st row until work is
140 cm (55 in) from beginning.
Rep from ** to ** of Pull-On
once.
Rep 1st row 5 times. Fasten
off.
Cut 96 lengths of C 45 cm (18 in)
long. With 4 strands make
12 tassels along both ends of
Scarf (see page 32).

TAMMY

Emu Fiord (50 g balls)

	Amount Required
Main Colour	1
Contrast	1
To fit an average adult head	

Aero crochet hook size 8·00 mm (No 00)

Tension
First 4 rounds measure 10 cm
(4 in) across.
To make a tension sample work
the first 4 rounds. Fasten off.
If your sample is not 10 cm
(4 in) across then refer to
Tension on page 25.

For abbreviations see page 25.

With M commence with 2 ch.
1st Round
8 dc into 2nd ch from hook.
2nd Round
2 dc into each dc, 1 ss into
first dc; 16 – dc. Leave yarn
behind work.
3rd Round
Attach C to same place as ss,
4 ch, 1 tr into same place as
join, * miss next dc, (1 tr,
1 ch, 1 tr) into next dc;
rep from * 6 times more, 1 ss
into 3rd of 4 ch. Leave yarn
behind work.
4th Round
Attach M to next 1 ch sp, 3 dc
into same place as join, * 1 dc
into next sp, 3 dc into next
1 ch sp; rep from * ending
with 1 dc into last sp, 1 dc
into first dc.
5th Round
1 dc into each dc, 1 ss into
first dc. Leave yarn behind work.
Rep last 3 rounds once more.
9th Round
Attach C to same place as ss,
4 ch, 1 tr into same place as
join, * miss next dc, (1 tr,
1 ch, 1 tr) into next dc, miss
2 dc, (1 tr, 1 ch, 1 tr) into
next dc, miss 2 dc, (1 tr,
1 ch, 1 tr) into next dc; rep
from * 6 times more, end with
miss next dc, (1 tr, 1 ch,
1 tr) into next dc, miss 2 dc,
(1 tr, 1 ch, 1 tr) into next
dc, miss 2 dc, 1 ss into 3rd
of 4 ch: 24 – groups. Leave
yarn behind work.
10th Round
Attach M to next 1 ch sp,
2 dc into same place as join,
* 1 dc into next sp, 2 dc into
next 1 ch sp; rep from *
ending with 1 dc into last sp,
1 dc into first dc: 72 – dc.
Rep 5th round once.
12th Round
Attach C to same place as ss,
4 ch, 1 tr into same place as
join, * miss 2 dc, (1 tr,
1 ch, 1 tr) into next dc; rep
from * ending with 1 ss into
3rd of 4 ch. Leave yarn behind work.
Rep 10th Round once.
14th Round
* 1 dc into each of next 3 dc,
miss next dc; rep from * 1 ss
into first dc: 54 – dc. Leave
yarn behind work.
Rep 12th Round once. Fasten off.
Rep 10th Round once.
17th Round
* miss next dc, 1 dc into each
of next 5 dc; rep from *
omitting 1 dc at end of last
rep, 1 dc into first dc.
18th Round
* miss next dc, 1 dc into each
of next 4 dc; rep from *
omitting 1 dc at end of last
rep, 1 ss into first dc. Fasten off.
With C make a pompon (see
page 32) and attach to centre
of Tammy.

HAT WITH BRIM

Emu Filigree (25 g balls) and
Emu Mix and Match DK (25 g balls)

Amount Required	D.K.	Filigree
	3	3

To fit an average head

Aero crochet hook size 4·50 mm (No 7)

Tension
12 sts or 6 Rounds to 10 cm (4 in).
To make a tension sample work the
first 6 Rounds. Fasten off.
  If your sample is not 10 cm
(4 in) across then refer to
Tension on page 25.

For abbreviations see pages 24 and
25.

With 1 strand of Filigree and
1 strand of D.K. used together
wrap yarn round finger once to
form a ring, then working in
continuous rounds throughout
make:–

1st Round
12 dc into commencing ring. Draw
ring tight.

2nd Round
(1 dc into next dc, 2 dc into
next dc) 6 times: 18 – dc.

3rd Round
(2 dc into next dc, 1 dc into
each of next 2 dc) 6 times:
24 – dc.

4th Round
(2 dc into next dc, 1 dc into
each of next 3 dc) 6 times:
30 – dc.

5th Round
(2 dc into next dc, 1 dc into
each of next 4 dc) 6 times:
36 – dc.

6th Round
(2 dc into next dc, 1 dc into
each of next 5 dc) 6 times:
42 – dc.

7th Round
(2 dc into next dc, 1 dc into
each of next 6 dc) 6 times:
48 – dc.

8th Round
(2 dc into next dc, 1 dc into
each of next 7 dc) 6 times:
54 – dc.

9th Round
(2 dc into next dc, 1 dc into
each of next 8 dc) 6 times:
60 – dc.

10th Round
(2 dc into next dc, 1 dc into
each of next 9 dc) 6 times:
66 – dc.

11th to 19th Rounds
1 dc into each dc.

20th Round
* 1 dc into each of next 2 dc,
leaving last lp of each dc on
hook make 1 dc into each of next
2 dc, yarn over hook and draw
through all lps on hook (a dec
formed); rep from * 15 times
more, 1 dc into each of next 2 dc.

21st Round
1 dc into each dc.

22nd Round
2 dc into each dc.

Next Rounds
1 dc into each dc until all
the Filigree is used, end with
1 ss into next dc. Fasten off.
  Use remaining D.K. to make
2 pompons (see page 32)
and attach to the Hat for
decoration. □

MOHAIR STOLE

Emu Filigree (25 g balls)

Amount Required	12	
	cm	in
Length	173	68
Width	46	18

Aero crochet hook size 7·00 mm (No 2)

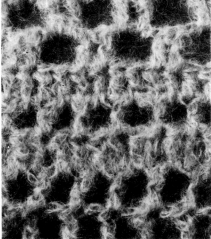

Tension
10 sts to 10 cm (4 in).
To make a tension sample commence with 14 ch, work as Stole for 5 rows. Fasten off.
If your sample is not 10 cm (4 in) across then refer to Tension on page 25.

For abbreviations see page 25.

Commence with 52 ch to measure 48 cm (19 in).
Foundation Row
1 tr into 6th ch from hook, * 1 ch, miss next ch, 1 tr into next ch; rep from * to end, turn: 24 – 1 ch sp.
1st Row
4 ch, miss first tr, * 1 tr into next tr, 1 ch; rep from * to within last 2 sts, end with 1 tr into 3rd of 4 ch, turn. Rep 1st row twice more.
**4th Row
3 ch, * 1 tr into next 1 ch sp, 1 tr into next tr; rep from * working 1 tr at end of last rep into 3rd of 4 ch, turn.
5th Row
4 ch, miss first 2 tr, * 1 tr into next tr, 1 ch, miss next tr; rep from * ending with 1 tr into 3rd of 3 ch, turn. Rep 4th row once.
7th Row
3 ch, miss first tr, 1 tr into next tr, * 2 ch, miss 2 tr, 1 tr into each of next 2 tr; rep from * to within last 3 sts, end with 2 ch, miss 2 tr, 1 tr into 3rd of 3 ch, turn.
8th Row
3 ch, 1 tr into first 2 ch sp, * 2 ch, 2 tr into next 2 ch sp; rep from * ending with 2 ch, 1 tr into 3rd of 3 ch, turn. Rep 8th row twice more.
11th Row
3 ch, * 2 tr into next 2 ch sp, 1 tr into each of next 2 tr; rep from * working 1 tr at end of last rep into 3rd of 3 ch, turn.
Rep 4th and 5th rows twice. **.
Rep 1st row an even No. of times until work is 127 cm (50 in) from beginning.
Rep from ** to ** once.
Rep 1st row 3 times, turn.

Edging

3 dc into first tr, (1 dc into next 1 ch sp, 1 dc into next tr) 23 times, 1 dc into last sp, 3 dc into 3rd of 4 ch (1st corner), along side make (2 dc, 3 ch, 1 ss into last dc) into each row-end, 2 dc into last row-end, 3 dc into 2nd corner, 1 dc into each ch, 3 dc into 3rd corner, along 2nd side make (2 dc, 3 ch, 1 ss into last dc) into each row-end, 2 dc into last row-end, 1 ss into first dc. Fasten off.
Cut remaining yarn into 46 cm (18 in) lengths and with 3 strands make a tassel (see page 32) into every alternate dc along both ends.

TRIANGULAR SHAWL

Patons Kismet (50 g balls)

Amount Required   7

Width excluding tassels   176 cm   (69 in)

Aero crochet hook size 4·50 mm (No 7)

Tension
5 patt to 10 cm (4 in).
To make a tension sample work the
first 5 rows. Fasten off.
  If your sample is not 10 cm
(4 in) across then refer to
Tension on page 25.

For abbreviations see page 25.

Working from lower edge up
commence with 6 ch, (3 tr,
1 ch, 1 dbl tr) into first ch
made, turn.

1st Row
5 ch, 3 tr into next 1 ch sp,
1 ch, 3 tr into sp formed by
turning ch, 1 ch, 1 dbl tr
into 4th of 5 ch, turn.

2nd Row
5 ch, (3 tr, 1 ch) into each
1 ch sp, 3 tr into sp formed
by turning ch, 1 ch, 1 dbl tr
into 4th of 5 ch, turn.
  Rep last row until Shawl
measures 153 cm (60 in) across.
(The weight of the tassels will
stretch this measurement to
176 cm (69 in) when Shawl is
completed.)

Last Row
1 dc into first dbl tr, * 1 dc
into next 1 ch sp, 3 ch, 1 ss
into last dc made (a picot
formed), 1 dc into each of next
2 tr; rep from * ending with
1 dc into next 1 ch sp, 3 ch,
1 ss into last dc made
(another picot formed), 1 dc
into 4th of 5 ch. Fasten off.
  Cut remaining yarn into 80 cm
(32 in) lengths and with 6 strands
make a tassel into every row-end
along both sides (see page 32).   □

SHAWL OF SHELLS

Templetons Shetland Fleece 4 ply (25 g balls)

	cm	in
Width	183	72
Depth	94	37
Amount Required	16	16

Aero crochet hook size 3·50 mm (No 9)

Tension
3 patt to 11·5 cm (4½ in).
To make a tension sample
commence with 28 ch, work as
for Shawl. Fasten off.
   If your sample is not 11·5 cm
(4½ in) across the top then refer
to Tension on page 25.

For abbreviations see page 25.

Working from top down commence
with 384 ch to measure 183 cm
(72 in).

Foundation Row
1 dc into 2nd ch from hook,
1 dc into each of next 2 ch,
* 6 ch, miss 5 ch, 1 dc into
each of next 3 ch; rep from
* to end, turn: 48 – 6 ch lps.

1st Patt Row
(2 tr, 3 ch, 1 ss into last
tr made (a picot formed), 5 tr,
3 ch, 1 ss into last tr made
(another picot formed), 2 tr)
all into each 5 ch lp to end,
1 dc into last dc, turn.

2nd Patt Row
Miss first dc, 1 ss into each
of next 3 tr, * 1 dc into each
of next 3 tr, 6 ch, miss 6 tr;
rep from * ending with 1 dc
into each of next 3 tr, turn:
1 – patt decreased.
   Rep 1st and 2nd patt rows 46
times, then 1st patt row once.
Fasten off: 1 – patt remains.

Edging

With right side facing attach
yarn to top corner, 1 dc into
same place as join, 1 dc into
each ch to end. Fasten off.
   Cut remaining yarn into 61 cm
(24 in) lengths and with 6 strands
make a tassel into every picot
along both side edges (see
page 32).
   Take 6 strands from each of
2 adjacent tassels and make a
knot 4 cm (1½ in) down (see
page 32). Continue all round.

CAR RUG AND CUSHION

Patons Beehive DK (50 g balls)

	Cushion		Car Rug	
	cm	in	cm	in
	40 × 40	16 × 16	127 × 165	50 × 65
Main Colour	2	2	9	9
1st Contrast	1	1	2	2
2nd Contrast	1	1	2	2
3rd Contrast	1	1	4	4
4th Contrast	1	1	7	7

Cushion Pad 40 × 40 16 × 16
2 button moulds
Aero crochet hook size 5·50 mm (No 5)

Tension
1 motif or 20 sts to 12·5 cm
(5 in).
Make 1 motif as a tension sample.
 If your motif is not 12·5 cm
(5 in) square then refer to
Tension on page 25.

For abbreviations see page 25.

Car Rug

Motif

With M commence with 4 ch,
1 ss into first ch to form a
ring.
1st Round
3 ch, 2 tr into commencing
ring, (1 ch, 3 tr into
commencing ring) 3 times, 1 ch,
1 ss into 3rd of 3 ch. Fasten
off.
2nd Round
Attach C 1 to any corner 1 ch sp,
3 ch, (2 tr, 1 ch, 3 tr) into
same place as join, (1 ch,
3 tr, 1 ch, 3 tr) into each of
next three 1 ch sp, 1 ch, 1 ss
into 3rd of 3 ch. Fasten off.
3rd Round
Attach C 2 to any corner 1 ch sp,
3 ch, (2 tr, 1 ch, 3 tr) into
same place as join, * 1 ch,
3 tr into next 1 ch sp, (1 ch,
3 tr) twice into corner 1 ch sp;
rep from * twice more, end with
1 ch, 3 tr into last 1 ch sp,
1 ch, 1 ss into 3rd of 3 ch.
Fasten off.
4th Round
Attach C 3 to any corner
1 ch sp, 3 ch, (2 tr, 1 ch,
3 tr) into same place as join,
* (1 ch, 3 tr) into each
1 ch sp to corner, (1 ch,
3 tr) twice into corner
1 ch sp; rep from * twice more
ending with (1 ch, 3 tr) into
each 1 ch sp, 1 ch, 1 ss into
3rd of 3 ch. Fasten off.
5th Round
With C 4 work as 4th Round.
Fasten off.
 Make 70 motifs altogether. Arrange
motifs into 7 strips of
10 motifs.
 Join by either sewing them
together with C 4 using an
over-sew stitch or by crocheting
them together as follows:—
Place the first 2 motifs together
with right sides facing inwards
then working through both attach
C 4 to first corner sp, 1 dc
into same place as join, 1 dc

continued overleaf

into each st to next corner,
1 dc into next corner sp.
Fasten off.
  Make all subsequent joinings in
the same manner.

Filling Strips (8 alike)

With M commence with 203 ch to
measure 128 cm (50½ in).
Foundation Row
1 tr into 4th ch from hook,
1 tr into each ch to end, turn:
201 – sts.
1st Row
3 ch, miss first tr, 1 tr into
each tr, 1 tr into 3rd of
3 ch, turn.
  Rep 1st row twice more. Fasten
off.
5th Row
Attach C 4 to first tr, 3 ch,
miss first 2 tr, * yarn over hook,
insert hook into next tr and
draw a lp up approximately
1 cm (½ in), (yarn over hook,
insert hook into same tr and
draw a lp up 1 cm (½ in))
3 times, yarn over hook and draw
through all lps on hook (a puff
st made), 1 ch, miss next tr;
rep from * ending with 1 tr
into 3rd of 3 ch. Fasten off
and turn.
6th Row
With M attach yarn to first tr,
3 ch, * 1 tr into next 1 ch sp,
1 tr into next puff st;
rep from * ending with 1 tr
into last puff st, 2 tr into
3rd of 3 ch, turn.
  Rep 1st row 3 times. Fasten off.
  Lay out the strips of motifs and
arrange them alternately with the
filling strips, beginning
and ending with a filling strip.
  Join strips together by either
sewing them or crocheting them
in the same way that was used
to join the motifs.

Edging

1st Round
With right side facing attach
M to any corner, then work dc
evenly round, 1 dc into first dc.
2nd Round
Make 1 dc into each dc end with
1 ss into first dc. Fasten off.

Cushion

Back and Front (both alike)

Work as for Car Rug motif until
4th Round is completed.

5th Round
With C 4 work as 4th Round.
**6th Round
With M work as 4th Round.
  Rep last Round once.
8th Round
With C 1 work as 4th Round.
9th Round
With C 2 work as 4th Round.
10th Round
With C 3 work as 4th Round.
11th Round
With C 4 work as 4th Round. ****.**
  Rep from ** to ** once more.
Rep 6th Round twice.

Edging

1st Round
Place Back and Front together
with right sides facing outwards
and Cushion pad inserted. Working
through both pieces attach M to
any st, 1 dc into same place
as join, 1 dc into each st
making 3 dc into each of the
4 corners, 1 dc into first dc.
2nd Round
Make 1 dc into each dc all
round working 3 dc into each
of the 4 corner dc, end with
1 ss into first dc. Fasten off.

CIRCULAR CLOTH, SET OF DOILIES AND LAMPSHADE

Twilleys Lyscordet (25 g balls)

	Amount Required	Diameter	
		cm	in
Circular Cloth	22	152	60
Large Doily	2	30	12
Medium Doily	1	20	8
Small Doily	1	10	4
Lampshade	7	30	12

Aero crochet hook size 3·00 mm (No 11)

Lampshade frame 30 cm (12 in) diameter

Tension
6 rounds to 5 cm (2 in).
To make a tension sample work
the first 6 rounds of Circular
Cloth. Fasten off.
  If your sample is not 5 cm
(2 in) across then refer to
Tension on page 25.

For abbreviations see page 25.

Circular Cloth

Commence with 4 ch, 1 ss into first ch to form a ring.

1st Round
4 ch, (1 tr into commencing ring, 1 ch) 9 times, 1 ss into 3rd of 4 ch: 10 – 1 ch sp.

2nd Round
1 ss into next 1 ch sp, 4 ch, 1 tr into same place as ss, 1 ch, (1 tr, 1 ch) twice into each 1 ch sp, 1 ss into 3rd of 4 ch: 20 – 1 ch sp.

3rd Round
1 dc into same place as ss, (2 dc into next 1 ch sp) 10 times, 3 dc into next 1 ch sp, 2 dc into each 1 ch sp, 1 ss into first dc: 42 – dc.

4th Round
5 ch, 1 tr into same place as ss, * 1 ch, miss next 2 dc, 6 tr into next dc (a shell formed), 1 ch, miss next 2 dc, (1 tr, 2 ch, 1 tr) into next dc; rep from * 5 times more ending with 1 ch, miss next 2 dc, 6 tr into next dc (another shell formed), 1 ch, 1 ss into 3rd of 5 ch: 7 – shells.

5th Round
1 ss into next 2 ch sp, 5 ch, 1 tr into same place as ss, * 1 ch, 6 tr into centre sp of next shell, 1 ch, (1 tr, 2 ch, 1 tr) into next 2 ch sp; rep from * ending with 1 ch, 6 tr into centre sp of last shell, 1 ch, 1 ss into 3rd of 5 ch.
Rep 5th Round once more.

7th Round
1 ss into next 2 ch sp, 5 ch, 1 tr into next sp, * 2 ch, miss next tr, 1 tr into next tr, 2 ch, 1 tr into centre sp of next shell, 2 ch, miss next tr, 1 tr into next tr, (2 ch, 1 tr into next sp) 3 times; rep from * ending with 2 ch, miss next tr, 1 tr into next tr, 2 ch, 1 tr into centre sp of next shell, 2 ch, miss next tr, 1 tr into next tr, 2 ch, 1 tr into last sp, 2 ch, 1 ss into 3rd of 5 ch.

8th Round
5 ch, * 1 tr into next tr, 2 ch; rep from * ending with 1 ss into 3rd of 5 ch: 42 – sp.

9th Round
* 2 dc into next 2 ch sp, (3 dc into next 2 ch sp) twice; rep from * ending with 1 ss into first dc: 112 – dc.

10th Round
5 ch, 1 tr into same place as ss, 1 ch, * miss next 3 dc, 6 tr into next dc, 1 ch, miss next 3 dc, (1 tr, 2 ch, 1 tr) into next dc, 1 ch; rep from * ending with miss 3 dc, 6 tr into next dc, 1 ch, 1 ss into 3rd of 5 ch: 14 – shells.
Rep 5th Round twice, 7th and 8th Rounds once: 84 – 2 ch sp.

15th Round
* (3 dc into next 2 ch sp, 2 dc into next 2 ch sp) twice, 2 dc into next 2 ch sp; rep from * 15 times more, (2 dc into next 2 ch sp) 4 times, 1 ss into first dc: 200 – dc.

16th Round
5 ch, 1 tr into same place as ss, 1 ch, * miss next 4 dc, 6 tr into next dc, miss next 4 dc, 1 ch, (1 tr, 2 ch, 1 tr) into next dc, 1 ch; rep from * ending with miss next 4 dc, 6 tr into next dc, 1 ch, 1 ss into 3rd of 5 ch: 20 – shells.
Rep 5th Round twice, 7th and 8th Rounds once: 120 – 2 ch sp.

21st Round
* 3 dc into next 2 ch sp, (2 dc into next 2 ch sp) twice; rep from * ending with 1 ss into first dc: 280 – dc.

22nd Round
As 16th Round: 28 – shells.
Rep 5th Round 3 times, 7th and 8th Rounds once: 168 – 2 ch sp.

28th Round
3 dc into next 2 ch sp, * 3 dc into next 2 ch sp, (2 dc into next 2 ch sp) 3 times; rep from * 19 times more, 3 dc into next 2 ch sp, ** 3 dc into next 2 ch sp, (2 dc into next 2 ch sp) 3 times; rep from ** 20 times more, 3 dc into next 2 ch sp, 2 dc into next 2 ch sp: 380 – dc.

29th Round
As 16th round: 38 – shells.
Rep 5th round 4 times, 7th and 8th rounds once: 228 – 2 ch sp.

36th Round
* 3 dc into next 2 ch sp, (2 dc into next 2 ch sp) 8 times; rep from * 23 times more, (2 dc into next 2 ch sp) 12 times, 1 ss into first dc: 480 – dc.

37th Round
As 16th round: 48 – shells.
Rep 5th round 5 times, 7th and 8th rounds once: 288 – 2 ch sp.

45th Round
* 3 dc into next 2 ch sp, (2 dc into next 2 ch sp)

70 times; rep from * 3 times more, (2 dc into next 2 ch sp) 4 times, 1 ss into first dc: 580 – dc.

46th Round
As 16th round: 58 – shells.
Rep 5th round 6 times, 7th and 8th rounds once: 348 – 2 ch sp.

55th Round
* 2 dc into each of next 20 two ch sp, 1 dc into next 2 ch sp; rep from * 15 times more, 2 dc into each of next 12 two ch sp, 1 ss into first dc: 680 – dc.

56th Round
As 16th round: 68 – shells.
Rep 5th round 7 times, 7th and 8th rounds once: 408 – 2 ch sp.

66th Round
* 2 dc into each of next 100 sp, 3 dc into next sp; rep from * 3 times more, end with 2 dc into each of last 4 sp, 1 ss into first dc: 820 – dc.

67th Round
As 16th round: 82 – shells.
Rep 5th round 8 times, 7th round once, 8th round 5 times: 492 – 2 ch sp.

82nd Round
1 ss into next 2 ch sp, * 12 ch, 4 dbl tr into 5th ch from hook, 5 ch, 1 ss into same place as last 4 dbl tr, 8 ch, miss next two 2 ch sp, 1 dc into next 2 ch sp; rep from * omitting 1 dc at end of last rep, 1 ss into first ch.
Fasten off.

Large Doily

Work as for Circular Cloth until 16th round is completed.
Rep 5th round twice.

Last Round
* (1 dc, 3 ch, 1 ss into last dc made, 1 dc) into next 2 ch sp, 1 ch, (5 tr, 3 ch, 1 ss into last tr made, 5 tr) into centre sp of next shell, 1 ch; rep from * ending with 1 ss into first dc. Fasten off.

Medium Doily

Work as for Circular Cloth until 10th round is completed.
Rep 5th round twice.
Rep last round of Large Doily once. Fasten off.

Small Doily

Work as for Circular Cloth until 5th round is completed.
Rep 5th round twice.

Rep last round of Large Doily
once. Fasten off.

Lampshade

Commence with 24 ch, 1 ss into
first ch to form a ring.
1st Round
3 ch, 35 tr into commencing
ring, 1 ss into 3rd of 3 ch:
36 – sts.
2nd Round
4 ch, * (1 tr, 1 ch) twice into
next tr, (1 tr, 1 ch) into
each of next 2 tr; rep from
* omitting 1 tr and 1 ch at
end of last rep, 1 ss into
3rd of 4 ch: 48 – sp.
3rd Round
4 ch, * 1 tr into next tr,
1 ch; rep from * 1 ss into 3rd
of 4 ch.
4th Round
2 dc into each 1 ch sp, 1 ss
into first dc.
   Rep 10th round of Circular Cloth
once: 12 – shells.
   Rep 5th round 5 times.
11th Round
5 ch, 1 tr into same place as
ss, 1 ch, * (1 tr, 2 ch,
1 tr) into next tr, 1 ch,
6 tr into centre sp of next
shell, 1 ch, miss 3 tr, (1 tr,
2 ch, 1 tr) into next tr,
1 ch; rep from * 10 times more,
end with (1 tr, 2 ch, 1 tr)
into next tr, 1 ch, 6 tr into
centre sp of last shell, 1 ch,
1 ss into 3rd of 5 ch.
12th Round
1 ss into next 2 ch sp, 5 ch,
1 tr into same place as ss,
1 ch, * 1 tr into next 1 ch sp,
1 ch, (1 tr, 2 ch, 1 tr)
into next 2 ch sp, 1 ch, 6 tr
into centre sp of next shell,
1 ch, (1 tr, 2 ch, 1 tr) into
next 2 ch sp, 1 ch; rep from
* 10 times more, end with 1 tr
into next 1 ch sp, 1 ch,
(1 tr, 2 ch, 1 tr) into next
2 ch sp, 1 ch, 6 tr into
centre sp of last shell, 1 ch,
1 ss into 3rd of 5 ch.
13th Round
1 ss into next 2 ch sp, 5 ch,
1 tr into same place as ss,
1 ch, * (1 tr, 2 ch, 1 tr)
into next single tr, 1 ch,
(1 tr, 2 ch, 1 tr) into next
2 ch sp, 1 ch, 6 tr into
centre sp of next shell, 1 ch,
(1 tr, 2 ch, 1 tr) into next
2 ch sp, 1 ch; rep from
* 10 times more, end with (1 tr,
2 ch, 1 tr) into last single
tr, 1 ch, (1 tr, 2 ch, 1 tr)

into next 2 ch sp, 1 ch, 6 tr
into centre sp of last shell,
1 ch, 1 ss into 3rd of 5 ch.
14th Round
1 ss into next 2 ch sp, 5 ch,
1 tr into same place as ss,
* (1 ch, 1 tr, 2 ch, 1 tr)
into each 2 ch sp, 1 ch, 6 tr
into centre sp of next shell;
rep from * ending with 1 ch,
1 ss into 3rd of 5 ch.
   Rep last round 15 times more.
30th Round
1 ss into next 2 ch sp, 5 ch,
1 tr into same place as ss,
* (1 tr, 2 ch, 1 tr) into each
2 ch sp, 6 tr into centre sp
of next shell; rep from * ending
with 1 ss into 3rd of 5 ch.
   Rep last round 7 times more.
38th Round
* 3 dc into each 2 ch sp, miss
next tr, 1 tr into each of next
6 tr; rep from * ending with
1 dc into first dc.
39th to 46th Rounds
Working in continuous round make
1 dc into each dc, 1 ss into
first dc. Fasten off.
   Cover the frame and sew 39th
roundto its lower edge making
sure that the shell lines cover
each vertical support.

Tassels

Cut remaining yarn into 36 cm
(14 in) lengths, with 3 strands
make a tassel into every dc on
last round (see page 32).

BEDSPREAD AND MATCHING CUSHION

Twilleys D.42 Health Vest Cotton (100 g hanks)

	Size		Amount
	cm	in	
Single Bedspread	200 × 300	78 × 120	33
Double Bedspread	245 × 300	96 × 120	41
Cushion	45 × 45	18 × 18	4

Aero crochet hook size 5·50 mm (No 5)
Cushion Pad 45 cm (18 in) square

Tension
1 motif to 23 cm (9 in) square.
Make 1 motif as a tension sample.
If your motif is not 23 cm
(9 in) square then refer to
Tension on page 25.

For abbreviations see
page 25.

Bedspread

Motif

Commence with 5 ch, 1 ss into
first ch to form a ring.
1st Round
12 dc into commencing ring,
1 ss into first dc.
2nd Round
3 ch, 3 tr into same place as
ss, remove lp from hook, insert
hook into 3rd of 3 ch and draw
dropped lp through, draw tight
(a popcorn formed), * 3 ch,
4 tr into next dc, remove lp
from hook, insert hook into top
of first tr and draw a lp
through, draw tight (another
popcorn made); rep from * ending
with 1 ch, 1 tr into top of
first popcorn: 12 – popcorns.
3rd Round
1 ch, * (5 ch, 1 dc into next
3 ch lp) twice, 7 ch, 1 dc
into next 3 ch lp; rep from
* twice more, end with (5 ch,
1 dc into next 3 ch lp) twice,
3 ch, 1 dbl tr into first ch
of this round.
4th Round
3 ch, 3 tr into top of dbl tr,
* (4 tr into centre ch of next
5 ch lp) twice, 7 tr into
centre ch of next 7 ch lp; rep
from * twice more, end with
(4 tr into centre ch of next
5 ch lp) twice, 3 tr into same
place as first 3 tr formed on
this round, 1 dc into 3rd of
3 ch.
5th Round
* 1 dc into each of next 14 tr,
2 dc into next tr; rep from
* twice more, end with 1 dc into
each of last 14 tr, 1 dc into
same place as first dc, 1 ss
into first dc.
6th Round
3 ch, 3 tr into same place as
ss, remove lp from hook, insert
hook into 3rd of 3 ch and draw
dropped lp through, draw tight
(a popcorn formed), 1 ch, a
popcorn into same place, * (1 ch,
miss next dc, a popcorn into
next dc) 7 times, miss next dc,
(1 ch, a popcorn) 3 times into
next dc; rep from * twice more,
end with (1 ch, miss next dc,
a popcorn into next dc) 7 times,
1 ch, miss next dc, a popcorn
into same place as ss, 1 ch,
1 ss into top of first popcorn.
7th Round
2 dc into same place as ss,
* (1 dc into next 1 ch sp,
1 dc into next popcorn) 9 times,

1 dc into next 1 ch sp, 3 dc
into next popcorn; rep from
* twice more, end with (1 dc
into next 1 ch sp, 1 dc into
next popcorn) 9 times, 1 ch,
1 dc into same place as first
2 dc, 1 ss into first dc.

Last Round
4 ch, 1 tr into same place as
ss, * (1 ch, miss next dc,
1 tr into next dc) 10 times,
miss next dc, (1 ch, 1 tr)
3 times into next dc; rep from
* twice more, end with (1 ch,
miss next dc, 1 tr into next
dc) 10 times, 1 ch, 1 tr into
same place as first tr, 1 ch,
1 ss into 3rd of 4 ch. Fasten
off.
 Make 84[108] motifs altogether.

Joining Motifs

Place 2 motifs together with
right sides facing outwards, then
working through both motifs
attach yarn to first sp, 1 dc
into same place as join, * (1 ch,
1 dc into next 1 ch sp)
12 times, 1 ch, place next
2 motifs together with right
sides facing outwards, 1 dc into
first sp; rep from * 10 times
more, end with (1 ch, 1 dc into
next 1 ch sp) 12 times. Fasten
off: 2 rows of 12 motifs have
been joined.
 Join 5[7] more rows of 12 motifs.
Join motifs sideways in the
same manner.

Edging

1st Round
With right side facing attach
yarn to any corner tr, 4 ch,
1 tr into same place as join,
** 1 ch, (1 tr into next tr,
1 ch) 13 times, * 1 tr into
centre corner tr of next motif,
(1 ch, 1 tr into next tr)
13 times; rep from * to next
corner, (1 ch, 1 tr) twice into
same place as last tr, **. Rep
from ** to ** twice more,
*** 1 ch, (1 tr into next tr,
1 ch) 13 times, 1 tr into
centre corner tr of next motif,
(1 ch, 1 tr into next tr)
13 times; rep from *** omitting
1 tr at end of last rep, (1 ch,
1 tr) twice into same place as
join, 1 ch, 1 ss into 3rd of
4 ch, turn.
2nd Round
4 ch, 1 tr into same place as
ss, * (1 ch, 1 tr) into each

tr to corner, (1 tr, 1 ch)
3 times into corner; rep from
* twice more, end with (1 ch,
1 tr) into each tr, 1 tr into
same place as join, 1 ss into
3rd of 4 ch.
 Rep 2nd round once more.
Last Round
* 2 dc into next 1 ch sp, 3 ch,
1 ss into last dc made; rep
from * 1 ss into first dc.
Fasten off.

Cushion

Back and Front (both alike)

Make 4 motifs as Bedspread.

Joining Motifs

Join 2 rows of 2 motifs as for
Bedspread.

Edging (worked on front only)

Work 1st and last rounds of
Bedspread Edging once.
 Complete by placing the Back and
Front together with right sides
facing outwards, insert the
cushion pad and sew together.

SEMI-CIRCULAR SHAWL

Jaeger 3 ply Pure Botany Wool (25 g balls)

Depth   90 cm (36 in)

Amount Required   11

Aero crochet hook size 4·00 mm (No 8)

Tension
22 sts to 9·5 cm (3¾ in).
To make a tension sample work the
first 5 rows. Fasten off.
  If your sample is not 10 cm
(4 in) across top then refer to
Tension on page 25.

For abbreviations see page 25.

Commence with 5 ch.
1st Row
(1 tr, 1 ch) 7 times into 5th
ch from hook, turn: 7 – 1 ch sp.
2nd Row
1 ss into first 1 ch sp, 4 ch,
* (1 tr, 1 ch) twice into next
1 ch sp; rep from * 4 times
more, 1 tr into last 1 ch sp,
turn: 11 – 1 ch sp.
3rd Row
1 ss into first 1 ch sp, 3 ch,
* (1 ch, 1 tr) twice into next
1 ch sp (an inc made), 1 ch,
1 tr into next 1 ch sp; rep
from * 4 times more, turn:
15 – 1 ch sp.
4th Row
1 ss into first 1 ch sp, 3 ch,
* (1 ch, 1 tr) twice into next
1 ch sp (an inc made), (1 ch,

1 tr) into each 1 ch sp until
next inc is reached; rep from
* 3 times more, end with (1 ch,
1 tr) twice into next 1 ch sp,
1 ch, 1 tr into last 1 ch sp,
turn: 4 – 1 ch sp increased.
  Rep last row until Shawl is
60 cm (24 in) from beginning.
Next Row
6 ch, * miss next 1 ch sp,
(3 tr, 4 ch, 3 tr) into next
1 ch sp, 2 ch, miss next
1 ch sp, 1 dbl tr into next
1 ch sp, 2 ch; rep from * to
within last 3 sp, end with miss
next 1 ch sp, (3 tr, 4 ch,
3 tr) into next 1 ch sp,
1 dbl tr into 3rd of 4 ch.
Next Row
4 ch, * (2 ch, 3 tr, 4 ch,
3 tr, 2 ch) into next 4 ch lp,
1 dbl tr into next dbl tr; rep
from * working 1 dbl tr at end
of last rep into 4th of 6 ch,
turn.
  Rep last row twice more.
Next Row
4 ch, * (2 ch, 4 tr, 4 ch,
4 tr, 2 ch) into next 4 ch lp,
1 dbl tr into next dbl tr; rep
from * working 1 dbl tr at end
of last rep into 4th of 6 ch,
turn.
  Rep last row 3 times more.
Next Row
4 ch, * (2 ch, 5 tr, 4 ch,
5 tr, 2 ch) into next 4 ch lp,
1 dbl tr into next dbl tr; rep
from * working 1 dbl tr at end
of last rep into 4th of 6 ch,
turn.
  Rep last row 3 times more.
Next Row
4 ch, * (2 ch, 6 tr, 4 ch,
6 tr, 2 ch) into next 4 ch lp,
1 dbl tr into next dbl tr; rep
from * working 1 dbl tr at end
of last rep into 4th of 6 ch,
turn.
  Rep last row 3 times more.
Next Row
4 ch, * (3 ch, 6 tr, 4 ch,
6 tr, 3 ch) into next 4 ch lp,
1 dbl tr into next dbl tr; rep
from * working 1 dbl tr at end
of last rep into 4th of 7 ch,
turn.
  Rep last row until Shawl is
90 cm (36 in) from beginning.

Edging

Working along side edge make
3 dc into each dbl tr row-end,
2 dc into each sp, 3 dc into
each dbl tr row-end at other
end. Fasten off.

EVENING BAG

Twilleys Lysbet (25 g balls)

Amount Required   2

Aero crochet hook size 3·50 mm (No 9)
2,000 Knitting Beads
Bag Frame 13 cm (5 in)

Tension
4 patt to 10·5 cm (4¼ in).
To make a tension sample
commence with 30 ch, work as
Bag for 13 rows. Fasten off.
  If your sample is not 10·5 cm
(4¼ in) across then refer to
Tension on page 25.

For abbreviations see page 25.

Back and Front (both alike)

Thread beads on to yarn.
Commence with 44 ch to measure
18 cm (7 in).
Foundation Row
1 dc into 2nd ch from hook,
(1 dc into next ch, 5 ch, miss
next 4 ch, 1 dc into each of
next 2 ch) 6 times, turn.
1st Row
1 dc into first dc, * 9 beaded
tr into next 5 ch lp, miss
next dc, 1 dc into next dc;
rep from * to end, turn.
2nd Row
6 ch, miss 3 beaded tr, * 1 dc
into each of next 3 beaded tr,
5 ch, miss 6 beaded tr; rep
from * ending with 1 dc into
each of next 3 beaded tr, 2 ch,
1 dbl tr into last dc, turn.
3rd Row
3 ch, 5 beaded tr into first
2 ch lp, * miss next dc, 1 dc
into next dc, 9 beaded tr into
next 5 ch lp; rep from * ending
with miss next dc, 1 dc into
next dc, 5 beaded tr into lp
formed by turning ch, 1 tr into
4th of 6 ch, turn.
4th Row
1 dc into each of next 2 beaded
tr, * 5 ch, miss 6 beaded tr,
1 dc into each of next 3 beaded
tr; rep from * ending with
5 ch, miss 6 beaded tr, 1 dc
into each of last 2 beaded tr,
turn.
  Rep last 4 rows 3 times more.
Rep 1st row once. Fasten off.
  Last row worked is the lower
edge of Bag. Join lower edge.
Join side seams leaving top 5 cm
(2 in) unsewn. Attach to frame and
line (see page 33).   □

RUG

Twilleys D.42 Cotton (100 g hanks)

	cm	in
Width	61	24
Length	122	48
Amount Required	9	9

Aero crochet hook size 4·50 mm (No 7)

Tension
11 sts to 10 cm (4 in).
To make a tension sample
commence with 12 ch, work 16
rows as Rug. Fasten off.
  If your sample is not 10 cm
(4 in) across then refer to
Tension on page 25.

For abbreviations see page 25.

Commence with 65 ch to measure
61 cm (24 in).

Foundation Row
1 dc into 2nd ch from hook,
1 dc into each ch to end, turn.

1st Row
1 dc into first dc,
* yarn round finger on left hand
to make a lp approx 4 cm
(1½ in), insert hook into next
dc and draw yarn through, yarn
over hook and draw through both
lps on hook (a loop st made),
1 dc into same dc; rep from
* to end, turn: 63 – loop sts.

2nd Row
1 dc into first dc, * miss
next st, 1 dc into next dc;
rep from * to end, turn.
  Rep 1st and 2nd rows until Rug
is 121 cm (47½ in) ending with
2nd row, turn.

Edging

Make 1 dc into each dc on last
row worked, 3 dc into corner,
1 dc into each row-end down side,
3 dc into next corner, 1 dc
into each ch, 3 dc into
corner, 1 dc into each row-end
up other side, 3 dc into last
corner, 1 ss into first dc.
Fasten off.

COLLAR AND CUFFS

Twilleys Lysbet (25 g balls)

Amount Required		2	
		cm	in
Length of Collar		39	15½
Length of Cuffs		20	8
Depth		6·5	2½

Aero crochet hook size 3·50 mm (No 9)

Tension
4 patt to 11·5 cm (4½ in).
To make a tension sample
commence with 34 ch, work as
for Cuffs to end. Fasten off.
  If your sample is not 11·5 cm
(4½ in) across then refer to
Tension on page 25.

For abbreviations see page 25.

Note

Instructions are given for Cuffs.
Figures in square brackets, [ ], refer
to Collar. Where only one figure is
given this refers to both.

Collar and Cuffs

Commence with 58[114] ch to
measure 20[39] cm (8[15½] in).
Adjust length here by working
an additional 8 ch for every
extra 3 cm (1⅛ in) required.

Foundation Row
1 dc into 2nd ch from hook,
1 dc into each ch to end, turn.

1st Row
5 ch, miss first 2 dc, 1 tr
into next dc, * 2 ch, miss next
dc, 1 tr into next dc; rep
from * to end, turn: 28[56] – sp.

2nd Row
1 dc into first tr, * 2 dc
into next sp, 1 dc into next
tr; rep from * ending with
2 dc into last sp formed by
turning ch, 1 dc into 3rd of
5 ch, turn.

3rd Row
1 dc into first dc, 1 dc into
each dc to end, turn.

4th Row
1 dc into first dc, * 3 ch,
miss next 5 dc, (a bullion st,
secure with 1 ch) 5 times into
next dc, 3 ch, miss 5 dc,
1 dc into next dc; rep from
* to end, turn: 7[14] – groups.

5th Row
7 ch, miss first 2 sp, 1 dc
into next sp, * 2 ch, 1 dc
into next sp, 4 ch, (1 tr,
2 ch, 1 tr) into next dc,
4 ch, miss next 2 sp, 1 dc
into next sp; rep from * ending
with 2 ch, 1 dc into next sp,
4 ch, 1 tr into last dc, turn.

6th Row
1 dc into first tr, * 3 ch,
(a bullion st, secure with
1 ch) 5 times into next 2 ch lp,
3 ch, 3 dc into next 2 ch sp;
rep from * omitting 3 dc at
end of last rep, 1 dc into 3rd
of 7 ch, turn.

7th Row
8 ch, miss first 2 sp, 1 dc
into next sp, * 2 ch, 1 dc
into next sp, 5 ch, miss next
dc, (1 tr, 2 ch, 1 tr) into
next dc, miss next 2 sp, 5 ch,
1 dc into next sp; rep from
* ending with 2 ch, 1 dc into
next sp, 5 ch, 1 tr into last
dc, turn.

continued overleaf

8th Row

1 dc into first tr, * 4 ch,
(a bullion st, secure with
1 ch) 5 times into next 2 ch lp,
4 ch, 3 dc into next 2 ch sp;
rep from * omitting 3 dc at end
of last rep, 1 dc into 3rd of
8 ch. Do not fasten off or turn.

Edging

(2 dc into next tr row-end,
1 dc into next dc row-end)
twice, 1 dc into each of next
2 dc row-ends, 2 dc into next
tr row-end, 3 dc into corner,
1 dc into each ch to within
last ch, 3 dc into next ch,
2 dc into next tr row-end,
1 dc into each of next 3 dc
row-ends, (2 dc into next tr
row-end, 1 dc into next dc
row-end) twice, * 6 dc into
next 4 ch lp, (3 ch, 1 ss into
last dc made, 2 dc into next
sp) 4 times, 3 ch, 1 ss into
last dc made, 6 dc into next
4 ch lp, miss next dc, 1 dc
into next dc; rep from * ending
with 6 dc into next 4 ch lp,
(3 ch, 1 ss into last dc made,
2 dc into next sp) 4 times,
3 ch, 1 ss into last dc made,
6 dc into last 4 ch lp, 1 dc
into last dc, 1 ss into first
dc. Fasten off.

MOTIF SHAWL

Patons Fiona (50 g balls)	
Amount Required	
Main Colour	7
5 Contrast Colours	1

Depth excluding tassels 81 cm (32 in)

Aero crochet hook size 4·50 mm (No 7)

Tension
1 motif to 18 cm (7 in) square.
Make 1 motif as a tension sample.
If your motif is not 18 cm
(7 in) square then refer to
Tension on page 25.

For abbreviations see page 25.

1st Motif

Centre Square

With any contrast colour commence
with 20 ch to measure 9 cm
(3½ in).

Foundation Row
1 tr into 6th ch from hook,
* 1 ch, miss next ch, 1 tr
into next ch; rep from * to
end, turn: 8 – 1 ch sp.

1st Row
4 ch, miss first tr, * 1 tr
into next tr, 1 ch; rep from
* ending with 1 tr into 3rd of
4 ch, turn.
Rep last row 6 times more.
Fasten off.

Edging

1st Round
Join M to corner, 3 dc into first sp, * 2 dc into each of next 3 sp, 10 ch, 1 dc into last dc made, turn lp just made and work into it 4 dc, (3 ch, 1 ss into last dc made, 3 dc) 3 times, 1 dc, turn lp back then continuing to work along square make 2 dc into each of next 3 sp, 5 dc into corner sp; rep from * 3 times more omitting 3 dc at end of last rep, 1 dc into first dc.

2nd Round
* 7 ch, 1 ss into 3rd ch from hook (a picot formed), 4 ch, 1 dc into 6th dc on next lp, 7 ch, 1 ss into 3rd ch from hook (another picot formed), 4 ch, miss 3 dc, 1 dc into next dc, 7 ch, 1 dc into 3rd ch from hook, 4 ch, 1 dc into centre dc at next corner; rep from * omitting 1 dc at end of last rep, 1 ss into first dc. Fasten off.

2nd Motif

Work as 1st Motif until 2nd round of Edging is reached.

2nd Round
7 ch, 1 ss into 3rd ch from hook (a picot formed), 4 ch, 1 dc into 6th dc on next lp, 5 ch, 1 dc into appropriate picot on 1st Motif, 1 ss into last ch made, 4 ch, miss 3 dc on 2nd Motif, 1 dc into next dc, 5 ch, 1 dc into appropriate picot on 1st Motif, 1 ss into last ch made, 4 ch, 1 dc into centre dc at next corner on 2nd Motif, 5 ch, 1 dc into appropriate picot on 1st Motif, 1 ss into last ch made, 4 ch, 1 dc into 7th dc on next lp on 2nd Motif, 5 ch, 1 dc into appropriate picot on 1st Motif, 1 ss into last ch made, 4 ch, miss 3 dc on 2nd Motif, 1 dc into next dc, complete as for 1st Motif. Fasten off.

Make 36 motifs in all and join to form the shape in diagram. Use a different contrast colour for each centre square.

Triangle Motif

Centre Rectangle

As 1st Motif until 4 rows are completed. Fasten off.

Edging

1st Row
Join M to corner at end of last row and make 4 ch. Fasten off. Rejoin M to corner at beginning of last row and make 6 ch, 1 dc into 3rd ch from hook (a picot formed), 3 dc into next ch, 3 ch, 1 ss into last dc made, 2 dc into each of next 2 ch, 2 dc into corner sp at beginning of last row, 2 dc into each of next 2 sp, 5 dc into corner sp at end of Foundation Row, 2 dc into each of next 3 sp, 10 ch, 1 dc into last dc made, turn lp just made and work into it 4 dc, (3 ch, 1 ss into 3rd ch from hook, 3 dc) 3 times, 1 dc, turn lp back then continuing to work along centre make 2 dc into each of next 3 sp, 5 dc into corner sp at beginning of Foundation Row, 2 dc into each of next 3 sp, into 4 ch length make 2 dc into each of next 2 ch, 3 ch, 1 ss into last dc made, 3 dc into next ch, 3 ch, 1 ss into last dc made, 1 dc into last ch. Fasten off.

2nd Row
Rejoin M to picot made at beginning of last row, 7 ch, 1 ss into 3rd ch from hook, 4 ch, miss 3 dc, 1 dc into next dc, 7 ch, 1 ss into 3rd ch from hook, 4 ch, 1 dc into corner dc, 7 ch, 1 ss into 3rd ch from hook, 4 ch, 1 dc into 7th dc on next lp, 7 ch, 1 ss into 3rd ch from hook, 4 ch, miss 3 dc, 1 dc into next dc, 7 ch, 1 ss into 3rd ch from hook, 1 dbl tr into last dc. Fasten off.

Make 8 more Triangular Motifs and sew into position across top as diagram.

Top Edging

1st Row
With wrong side facing attach M to corner picot, 1 dc into same place as join, 1 dc into next ch, * 1 dc into each of next 4 sts, (1 dc into next sp, 1 dc into next st) 8 times, 1 dc into each of next 4 sts, 1 dc into each of next 3 ch, 1 dc into next st, 1 dc into each of next 3 ch; rep from * 9 times more, ending with 1 dc into next ch, 1 dc into corner picot, turn.

2nd Row
1 dc into first dc, * 3 ch, 1 ss into last dc made, 1 dc into each of next 3 dc; rep from * to end. Fasten off.

Tassels

Cut remaining M into 45 cm (18 in) lengths and with 6 strands make a tassel (see page 32) into every picot and dc along both side edges. □

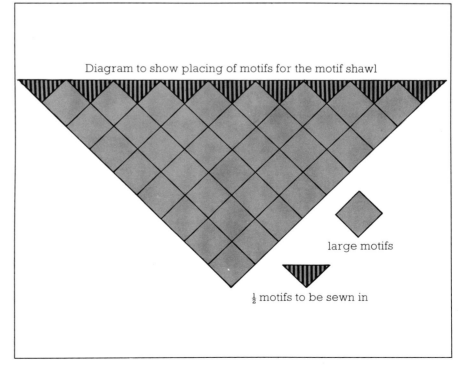

Diagram to show placing of motifs for the motif shawl

large motifs

½ motifs to be sewn in

Left The honey colour of the Hat with Brim will suit almost any complexion. The pattern is on p. 97. Here it is worn with the Mohair Shawl; pattern on p. 98.

Above The Car Rug and Cushion (pattern on p. 95) have been made up in five warm shades, ranging from cream to dark brown.

Below The Pull-on and Scarf (pattern on p. 101) in thick, pure wool can keep out the coldest winter winds. Colours for the Tammy (pattern on p. 96) can be chosen to contrast with or match a favourite sweater.

ROUND CUSHION AND BOLSTER

Sirdar Super Wash 4 ply (25 g balls)
or
Sirdar Super Wash DK (25 g balls)

Amount Required	Round Cushion		Bolster
	4 ply	D.K.	4 ply
Main Colour	6	6	6
Contrast	4	5	2
Aero crochet hook size	4·00 mm (No 8)	5·00 mm (No 6)	4·00 mm (No 8)

Cushion Pad	cm	in	cm	in
	45 × 3	18 × 3	45 × 18	18 × 7

2 large button moulds

Tension
4 ply version first 4 rounds
measure 10 cm (4 in) across.
DK version first 4 rounds
measure 12·5 cm (5 in) across.
If the measurement is not correct
refer to Tension on page 25.

For abbreviations see page 25.

4 ply Round Cushion

1st Side
With C commence with 6 ch,
1 ss into first ch to form a
ring.

1st Round
3 ch, 23 tr into ring, 1 ss
into 3rd of 3 ch. Fasten off.

2nd Round
Attach M to same place as ss,
3 ch, * miss 2 tr, (1 tr,
3 ch, 1 tr) into next tr; rep
from * 6 times more ending with
1 tr into same place as join,
3 ch, 1 ss into 3rd of 3 ch.

3rd Round
1 dc into next sp between
2 sts, * (3 tr, 1 ch, 3 tr)
all into next 3 ch sp, 1 dc
into next sp between tr; rep
from * working 1 dc at end of
last rep into first dc.

4th Round
* 8 tr into next 1 ch sp, 1 dc
into next dc; rep from *
omitting 1 dc at end of last
rep, 1 ss into first dc.
Fasten off.

5th Round
Attach C to centre sp of any
8 tr group, 1 dc into same
place as join, * 3 ch, 1 tr
into next dc, 4 ch, 1 dc into
centre sp of next group; rep
from * omitting 1 dc at end of
last rep, 1 ss into first dc:
72 − sts.

6th Round
3 ch, 1 tr into each st, 1 ss
into 3rd of 3 ch. Fasten off.

7th Round
Attach M to same place as ss,
3 ch, * miss 3 tr, (1 tr,
3 ch, 1 tr) all into next tr;
rep from * ending with 1 tr
into same place as join, 3 ch,
1 ss into 3rd of 3 ch.
Rep 3rd and 4th rounds once:
18 − groups.

10th Round
Attach C to centre sp of any
8 tr group, 1 dc into same
place as join, * 3 ch, 1 tr
into next dc, 3 ch, 1 dc into
centre sp of next group, 2 ch,
1 tr into next dc, 3 ch, 1 dc
into centre sp of next group;

rep from * 8 times more omitting
1 dc at end of last rep, 1 ss
into first dc: 135 – sts.
  Rep 6th round once.

12th Round
Attach M to same place as ss,
3 ch, * miss 4 tr, (1 tr,
3 ch, 1 tr) into next tr; rep
from * ending with 1 tr into
same place as join, 3 ch, 1 ss
into 3rd of 3 ch.
  Rep 3rd and 4th rounds once:
27 – groups.

15th Round
Attach C to centre sp of any
8 tr group, 1 dc into same
place as join, * 2 ch, 1 tr
into next dc, 2 ch, 1 dc into
centre sp of next group, (2 ch,
1 tr into next dc, 3 ch, 1 dc
into centre sp of next group)
twice; rep from * 8 times more
omitting 1 dc at end of last
rep, 1 ss into first dc:
180 – sts.
  Rep 6th, 12th, 3rd and 4th rounds
once: 36 – groups.

20th Round
Attach C to centre sp of any
8 tr group, 1 dc into same
place as join, * (2 ch, 1 tr
into next dc, 2 ch, 1 dc into
centre sp of next group) 3 times,
2 ch, 1 tr into next dc,
3 ch, 1 dc into centre sp of
next group; rep from * 8 times
more omitting 1 dc at end of
last rep, 1 ss into first dc:
225 – sts.
  Rep 6th, 12th, 3rd and 4th rounds
once: 45 – groups.

25th Round
Attach C to centre sp of any
8 tr group, 1 dc into same
place as join, * 2 ch, 1 tr
into next dc, 2 ch, 1 dc into
centre sp of next 8 tr group;
rep from * omitting 1 dc at end
of last rep, 1 ss into first
dc: 270 – sts.

26th Round
Working into front lps only make
1 dc into same place as ss,
* 3 ch, 1 ss into last dc made,
1 dc into each of next 5 sts;
rep from * omitting 1 dc at end
of last rep, 1 ss into first
dc. Fasten off.

2nd Side

As 1st Side until 26th round is
completed. Do not fasten off.

**Gusset

Next Round
Working into remaining back lps
of sts make 3 ch, 1 tr into
each lp, 1 ss into 3rd of 3 ch.

Next Round
3 ch, 1 tr into each tr, 1 ss
into 3rd of 3 ch.
  Rep last round until gusset
is 7 cm (2½ in) from beginning.
Fasten off.
  Carefully sew the 2 pieces
together with the pad inserted.
  With M cover 2 buttons (see
page 00), sew these to centre
of cushion, one on each side. **

DK Round Cushion

1st Side
As 1st Side of 4 ply Round
Cushion until 20th round is
completed.
  Rep 26th round once.

2nd Side
As 1st Side of 4 ply Round
Cushion until 20th round is
completed.
  Rep 26th round once. Do not fasten
off. Rep from ** to ** of 4 ply
Round Cushion once.

Bolster

1st Side
As 1st Side of 4 ply Round
Cushion until 10th round is
completed.
  Rep 6th round once. Do not
fasten off.
  Rep 26th round once. Fasten off.

2nd Side
As 1st Side of 4 ply Round
Cushion until 10th round is
completed.
  Rep 6th round once. Do not
fasten off.
  Rep 26th round once. Fasten off.

13th Round
Working into remaining lps of
tr, attach M to any tr, 1 dc
into same place as join, * 1 dc
into each of next 4 tr, miss
next tr; rep from * omitting
1 dc at end of last rep: 108 – dc.

Next Rounds
Working in continuous rounds
into back lps only, make 1 dc
into each dc, until work is
45 cm (18 in) from 13th round,
end last round with 1 ss into
first dc. Fasten off.
  Join the 2 pieces together
inserting cushion pad.

Tassels (both alike)
With 2 strands of M make 15 ch
Fasten off.
  Cut fifteen 25 cm (10 in) lengths of M

and make a tassel into last ch (see
page 32).
  Make a bobble (see page 32)
and thread the chain length
through it so that the bobble
covers the top of the tassel.
Sew into position.
  Sew the tassels to centre, at
either end of cushion. Pass the
needle right through the cushion
and secure tightly. (Use a long
mattress needle.)

Left Soft, natural cotton is ideal for a bedside rug. The pattern can be found on p. 110.

Right The matching Bedspread and Cushion entails quite a lot of work but will give pleasure for many years. the pattern is on p. 106.

Below Every home has room for some bright scatter cushions. **From Left to Right:** Round Cushion (pattern on p. 116); Rectangular Cushion (pattern on p. 120); Bolster (pattern on p. 116) and Patchwork Cushion (pattern on p. 121).

Rectangular Cushion

Sirdar Super Wash DK (25 g balls)

Amount Required
Main Colour 5
Contrast   4

Aero crochet hook size 5·50 mm   (No 5)
Cushion Pad 35 × 55 cm   (13½ × 21½ in)
4 large button moulds

Tension
13 sts to 10 cm (4 in).
To make a tension sample
commence with 15 ch, work as
back for 11 rows. Fasten off.
  If your sample is not 10 cm
(4 in) across then refer to
Tension on page 25.

For abbreviations see page 25.

Back

With M commence with 75 ch to
measure 55 cm (21½ in).

Foundation Row
1 tr into 3rd ch from hook,
* miss next ch, 1 dc into next
ch, miss next ch, 3 tr into
next ch; rep from *
omitting 1 tr at end of last
rep, turn: 17 – 3 tr groups.

1st Patt Row
Attach C to first tr, 1 dc
into same place as join, * 3 tr
into next dc, miss next tr,
1 dc into next tr; rep from
* working 1 dc at end of last
rep into 3rd of 3 ch. Do not
turn.

2nd Patt Row
Attach M to first dc, 3 ch,
1 tr into same place as join,
* miss next tr, 1 dc into next
tr, 3 tr into next dc; rep
from * omitting 1 tr at end of
last rep, turn.
  Rep last 2 rows until work is
35 cm (13½ in) ending with 2nd
patt row. **.
  Fasten off both colours.

Front

As Back to **. Fasten off C only.

Edging

1st Round
With M make 1 dc into each st
across top, 3 dc into corner,
2 dc into first row-end, (1 dc
into next row-end, 2 dc into
next row-end); rep from * down
side to next corner, 3 dc into
corner, 1 dc into each ch along
lower edge, 3 dc into corner,
work along 2nd side to match
first side, 3 dc into corner,
1 dc into first dc.

2nd to 4th Rounds
Working in continuous rounds
make * 1 dc into each dc until
2nd dc of corner group is
reached, 3 dc into next dc;
rep from * ending last round
with 1 ss into first dc. Fasten
off.
  Sew the 2 pieces together leaving
edging loose and inserting
cushion pad.
  Cover 4 buttons (see page
32) and sewing right through
the cushion sew one on the front
and one on the back 15 cm (6 in)
from side edge. Attach the other
two in the same manner 15 cm
(6 in) from other side edge.

PATCHWORK CUSHION

Emu Scotch Superwash DK (25 g balls)

Amount Required	
Main Colour	4
1st Contrast	2
2nd Contrast	3
3rd Contrast	2
4th Contrast	2

Aero crochet hook size 4·50 mm (No 7)
45 cm (18 in) square cushion pad

Tension
1 motif to 11 cm (4½ in) square.
To make a tension sample make
1 motif.
  If your motif is not 11 cm (4½ in)
square then refer to Tension on
page 25.

For abbreviations see page 25.

Back and Front (both alike)

1st Motif
With C 1 commence with 18 ch to
measure 11 cm (4½ in).
Foundation Row
1 dc into 2nd ch from hook,

1 dc into each ch to end, turn:
17 – dc.
1st Row
1 dc into first dc, 1 dc into
each dc to end, turn.
2nd Row
1 dc into first dc, 1 dc into
each dc to end. Fasten off and
turn.
3rd Row
Attach C 2 to first dc, 1 dc
into same place as join, 1 dc
into each dc to end, turn.
4th Row
3 ch, miss first dc, * 4 tr
into next dc, remove lp from
hook, insert hook into top of
first tr made and draw dropped
lp through, secure with 1 ch
(a popcorn made), miss next dc;
rep from * 6 times more, end
with 1 popcorn into next dc,
1 tr into last dc, turn.
5th Row
1 dc into first tr, (1 dc into
next popcorn, 1 dc into next
1 ch sp) 7 times, 1 dc into
next popcorn, 1 dc into 3rd of
3 ch. Fasten off and turn:
17 – dc.
  With C 3 rep 3rd, 1st and 2nd
rows once.
  With M rep 3rd, 4th and 5th rows
once.
  With C 4 rep 3rd, 1st and 2nd
rows once.
  Make 15 more motifs.
  Lay out the motifs into 4 rows
of 4, with the lines of colour
of each motif running vertically
or horizontally, alternating
along the row. Sew into position.

Edging (worked only on Front)

1st Round
With right side facing attach M
to any corner, 3 dc into same
place as join, then work (17 dc
across each of next 4 motifs,
3 dc into next corner) 3 times,
17 dc across each of next
4 motifs, 1 dc into first dc.
2nd Round
3 dc into next dc, (1 dc into
each dc until 2nd dc at corner
is reached, 3 dc into next dc)
3 times, 1 dc into each dc,
1 dc into first dc.
Last Round
* 3 ch, 1 ss into last dc made,
1 dc into each of next 3 dc;
rep from * ending with 1 ss into
first dc. Fasten off.
  Sew back and front together
inserting the cushion pad.

Below The Set of Doilies (pattern on p. 103) is set off by otherwise plain tableware.

Right The large Circular Tablecloth and Lampshade are made from the same basic pattern as the doilies (p. 103). See also the back jacket of the book.

Far Right The delicate tracery of the motif Tablecloth (pattern on p. 124) is not as difficult as it looks to crochet.

MOTIF TABLECLOTH

Coats Mercer Crochet No 40 (20 g balls)

Measurement   91 × 91 cm (36 × 36 in)

Amount Required   12

Milward steel crochet hook size 1·00 mm (No 4)

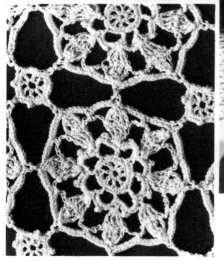

Tension

1 large motif to 7·5 cm (3 in).
Make 1 large motif as a tension
sample.

   If your motif is not 7·5 cm
(3 in) across then refer to
Tension on page 25.

For abbreviations see page 25.

1st Large Motif

Thread round finger to form a
ring.

1st Round

5 ch, (1 tr, 2 ch) 7 times
into ring, 1 ss into 3rd of
5 ch. Draw commencing ring tight.

2nd Round

1 dc into same place as ss,
* 2 dc into next sp,
1 dc into next tr;
rep from * 6 times more, 2 dc
into next sp, 1 ss into first
dc.

3rd Round

1 dc into same place as ss,
* 5 ch, miss 2 dc, 1 dc into
next dc; rep from * 6 times
more, 5 ch, miss 2 dc, 1 ss
into first dc.

4th Round

(4 dc, 3 ch, 4 dc) into each
5 ch lp, end with 1 ss into
first dc 8 – petals.

5th Round

4 ch, 3 dbl tr into same place
as ss, * 5 ch, 4 dbl tr into
sp between next 2 petals; rep
from * ending with 5 ch, 1 ss
into 4th of 4 ch.

6th Round

4 ch, leaving last lp on hook
make 1 dbl tr into each of next
3 dbl tr, thread over hook and
draw through all lps on hook (a
cluster formed), * 4 ch, 1 dc
into next 5 ch lp, 4 ch,
a 4 dbl tr cluster over next
4 dbl tr; rep from * ending
with 4 ch, 1 dc into next
5 ch lp, 4 ch, 1 ss into top
of first cluster.

7th Round

* 7 dc into each of next 2 lps,
3 ch; rep from * ending with
1 ss into first dc. Fasten off.

2nd Large Motif

Work as 1st Large Motif until
7th round is reached.

7th Round

7 dc into each of next 2 lps,
1 ch, 1 dc into and 3 ch lp
on 1st Motif, 1 ch, 7 dc into
each of next 2 lps on 2nd Motif,
now complete as 1st Motif.
Fasten off.

   Make a square of motifs
with twelve along
each side.

Filling Motif

Work as for 1st Large Motif
until 2nd round is reached.

2nd Round

1 dc into same place as ss,
2 dc into next sp, 1 dc into
next tr, 1 ch, 1 dc into
appropriate 3 ch lp on a motif,
* 1 ch, 1 dc into same tr on
filling motif, 2 dc into next
sp, 1 dc into next tr, 3 ch,
1 dc into same tr, 2 dc into
next sp, 1 ch, 1 dc into
3 ch lp on next motif; rep from
* ending with 1 ch, 1 ss into
first dc on Filling Motif.
Fasten off.

   Work a Filling Motif into each gap. □

INDEX